Coming Back to a Peaceful Life:

For Recovering Gamblers

Coming Back to a Peaceful Life

FOR RECOVERING GAMBLERS

~

Mike Marcotte
and Charlynn Robertson

Intërieur Publishing
Minneapolis, Minnesota

Published by: Intërieur Publishing, 6008 Abbott Avenue South, Suite 100, Edina, MN 55410.
Cover photo © Digital Vision, Inc.
Book design: Dorie McClelland, Spring Book Design
Printed in USA

Publisher's Cataloging-in-Publication
(Provided by Quality Books, Inc.)

Marcotte, Mike.
Coming back to a peaceful life : for recovering gamblers / Mike Marcotte and Charlynn Robertson.
p. cm.
Includes index.
ISBN 0-9721323-0-9
1. Compulsive gamblers--Prayer-books and devotions.
2. Twelve-step programs--Religious aspects--Meditations.
3. Devotional calendars. I. Robertson, Charlynn.
II. Title.

BL625.9.C65M37 2002 291.4'32
QBI02-200560

A portion of the proceeds from the sale of this book will go towards assisting recovering gamblers and their families.

THIS BOOK IS DEDICATED TO THE CELEBRATION OF THE LIFE OF

Michael J. Marcotte
January 12. 1943–June 28, 2002

StarTribune, July 3, 2002

Obituary: Michael Marcotte, 59; helped compulsive gamglers

Jeff McMillan, Star Tribune

Sondra Mattox was doing research on addiction when Michael Marcotte helped her realize that she was an addict herself.

She entered treatment in 1996 at the Intervention Institute/Gamblers Choice Program in northeast Minneapolis, which Marcotte had cofounded. With Marcotte facilitating her journey away from her gambling addiction, Mattox made a new start.

"He helped me to really understand addiction from a whole different light," said Mattox, a psychologist and now a treatment supervisor at the institute. "Addiction is a disease that can cut across any and all walks of life."

Marcotte, who overcame his own addictions to start the Intervention Institute in 1985, died of heart disease Friday at his home in St. Louis Park. He was 59.

He grew up in West St. Paul, graduated from Sibley High School and was a Navy frogman from 1962 to '66, stationed in Iceland. He worked as a line repairman for Northwestern Bell.

In 1975, realizing that he was losing control of his life to alcoholism and gambling, he entered treatment.

Sober and free of his compulsive gambling, he sought higher education in addiction treatment, getting an associate's degree and taking classes at Hamline and Metropolitan State universities.

His passion for helping others turned into the Intervention Institute, which he started with his wife at the time, Susan. They had met while in treatment.

It started out with a dual focus on alcoholism and gambling addiction, but became more gambling-oriented in 1992. It remains among a handful of centers in the state that treat gambling addiction.

"I don't use the word 'pioneer' very loosely, but he has definitely been a pioneer in this field," Mattox said.

Marcotte, not content just to supply his clients with group therapy and counseling, had big plans to help even more addicts. Among his hopes were providing transitional housing, inpatient treatment and financial planning advice for compulsive gamblers.

"His legacy will live on; we're going to make sure of that," said Susan Marcotte, the institute's acting executive director. "By the lives that he touched, he will never be forgotten."

Endorsement from Leonard Prescott

Responsibility is the foundation of the Native American population. In every business transaction we undertake, we go to great lengths to ensure our integrity towards that foundation is perpetuated.

With this in mind, gaming was originally established by Native Americans as a means to build and support the community. Significant good has been done with the development of responsible gaming businesses. For one, it allowed Native Americans to provide jobs for both Native Americans and non-Native Americans. It also built schools to provide a solid education for children. And, it provided housing which, in turn, provided stability for families, allowing them to establish individual family foundations to build upon.

Along with this social good that we provided, we recognized that while the gaming business itself was not a problem, there were a few unfortunate individuals whose lives were out of control due to significant ongoing problems with compulsive gambling. We knew there was something we could and wanted to do to help.

Subsequently, Mike Marcotte and I developed training for gaming employees to assist them in identifying compulsive gamblers and, if requested, offer support. We also established a compulsive gambling treatment scholarship program for gaming guests, funded by my tribe. This was not a handout, but a commitment to assist compulsive gamblers who were serious in getting some help for their problem. I believe this was the first and most significant joint effort between a gaming business and a compulsive treatment provider in the history of Native American gaming or the private gaming industry.

Our commitment to responsible gaming reinforced the integrity and continuing social good of our tribe. It created a bridge between the gaming business and those who would criticize the gaming business and the market it serves.

I wish to extend my sincere hope for you, as you travel on your journey, that you find the peace and serenity freedom from compulsive gambling can bring you.

My Best Regards,
LEONARD PRESCOTT
Chairman
Eaglevisions

Acknowledgments

I would like to acknowledge all the individuals who are dealing with the powerful addiction of gambling. Also those yet to come to this addiction.

It is my desire that this daily reader will help in the day-to-day living and in focusing on the present as today is all we have.

Just for today I chose not to gamble.

MIKE MARCOTTE

This is more than a daily reader for me. It has been a journey that many people have participated in along the way. It has been an honor for me to take their belief in me and produce this book. Audrae Diestler, you've taught me so much, particularly about unconditional love. Ann Ruschy, you are precious to me. Jo, Beki and Adam Carr; Zach, Dan, Stephanie and Mike Robertson; Jon, Chelsey and Jessica Radermacher; Kristi, Nathan and Ryan Anderson; Kari, Nicholas and Chris Kern; Darren, Sarah, and Emily Ruschy. Wes Hamilton, Lori Palm, Cindy Jamieson, Anne Westfall, what an incredible journey we're on. Jan and Gary Quick; thick and thin, we've been through it all. Dick Cottrell; you believed in me even when I couldn't. Dave Teckman, you make me a better person just by your friendship. My writing partner, Mike Marcotte; we made it happen. Sue Maher; I will never forget you.

CHARLYNN ROBERTSON

"Keep the faith."

Mike Marcotte

Introduction

Compulsive gambling is sometimes called the hidden or secret disease. The readings prepared for this book are intended to assist our readers in releasing those secrets and to reinforce their personal recovery process. In doing so, we have attempted to incorporate each of the Twelve Steps of the Compulsive Gambler's Recovery Program into the readings.

We recognize that no one source has all the answers. In the recovery process, each of us draws from many—books, groups, formal treatment programs, family members and friends. Most importantly, we draw from within ourselves and our commitment to our recovery from compulsive gambling.

We, too, have brought many sources into the readings. Some are famous, some are not. Each in some way has something to say.

Consequently, the readings have different meanings in readers lives depending on their own place in the recovery process. What doesn't fit today may fit tomorrow, next month or next year.

We personally need to decide what does fit for us in each reading. As in other Twelve Step programs, "take what you can use and leave the rest." The important thing is to keep reading, working on our recovery program and growing.

The stakes are high in the recovery process. So are the rewards. It is the only sure bet we will ever make. Through recovery and self-acceptance, the outcome is determined. Our lives will be filled with serenity, peace of mind, joy and happiness.

Recovery is a personal journey, but the process involves the support of others. We are thankful for our own recovery processes using Twelve Step programs. It is our hope that each reader will find the peace, joy and serenity in their recovery program that we are finding in ours.

The Serenity Prayer

God grant me the serenity
To accept the things
I cannot change,
The courage to change
The things I can,
And the wisdom to know the difference.

The Twelve Steps

1.

We admitted we were powerless over gambling—that our lives had become unmanageable.

2.

Came to believe that a Power greater than ourselves could restore us to a normal way of thinking and believing.

3.

Made a decision to turn our will and our lives over to the care of this power of our own understanding.

4.

Made a searching and fearless moral and financial inventory of ourselves.

5.

Admitted to ourselves and to another human being the exact nature of our wrongs.

6.

Were entirely ready to have these defects of character removed.

7.

Humbly asked God of our understanding to remove our shortcomings.

8.

Made a list of all persons we had harmed and became willing to make amends to all.

9.

Made direct amends to such people wherever possible, except when to do so would injure them or others.

10.

Continued to take personal inventory and when we were wrong, promptly admitted it.

11.

Sought through prayer and meditation to improve our conscious contact with God as we understood Him, praying only for knowledge of His will for us and the power to carry that out.

12.

Having made an effort to practice these principles in all our affairs, we tried to carry this message to other compulsive gamblers.

January 1

The worst thing in your life may contain seeds of the best.
When you can see crisis as an opportunity,
your life becomes not easier, but more satisfying.

JOE KOGEL

We hit our bottom. It was the worst thing that ever happened to us. We didn't know how we could go on. We could see no future for ourselves. It was a major crisis.

Out of this crisis came opportunity for us. How, we may ask? Well, before our crisis, we had no hope. The crisis forced us to look at our compulsive gambling addiction and admit things were out of control. It got us involved in our recovery. Today, we are free of compulsive gambling behavior and are working our program to stay that way.

~

I am thankful for the opportunity to be free from compulsive gambling. I am thankful for the recovery program I am working.

January 2

Speak not against anyone whose burden you have not weighed yourself.

MARION BRADLEY

It is easy to judge others' behaviors and situations. Looking in from the outside, we can see a number of possibilities for them. Why haven't they looked at it this way? What is wrong with trying that idea?

What we must remember is we don't really know all that is going on with these people. We don't have all the details. Maybe we don't have any business knowing. So, we must remember to keep our thoughts and advice to ourselves. To judge others is to be using energy we should be using to work our own program, which teaches us not to judge.

Today I will ensure that I am working
my own recovery program
and not judging others' actions.

January 3

The man who is waiting for something to turn up
might start on his shirt sleeves.
GARTH HENRICHS

Recovery isn't something that is just handed to us. To be truly successful in our program, we have to work it each step of the way. That means learning about ourselves, our addiction and our hope in recovery. We need to roll up our sleeves and dive into the process of recovery. At times it may seem awkward to us because the behaviors that go with recovery are unfamiliar to us. We need to trust the process and practice those behaviors until they are our own. Once we own the recovery behaviors and believe in them, we grow in our recovery process.

~

I will work my program to the best of my ability today.
I will continue to grow.

January 4

A man's not finished when he's defeated; he's finished when he quits.

RICHARD NIXON

At times, recovery may seem difficult. Perhaps we feel we should be able to make faster progress in our program. We want to bound through the 12 steps at break neck speed and "be cured" from our gambling compulsion. We are impatient with the slower, steady improvement we are showing.

This kind of thinking can get us into trouble. We may decide to quit our program and work on our own. For a while—a very short while—things seem just fine. Then trouble sets in. We may slip and return to compulsive gambling. Without the support of our recovery program, we may stay caught in the web of compulsive gambling.

Recovery isn't about speed. It is about learning and changing our behavior so we can live a life of peace and serenity.

~

I am thankful for the life I have found in recovery.
When the going seems to be slow,
I will remember serenity means steady progress, not a race.

January 5

I don't have all the answers. I have all the questions.

ALICIA

How can I earn back the trust of those I've harmed? How can I be sure I won't gamble again? These are some of the questions that surfaced in Alicia's recovery program. She has a hunger for making sure she does everything perfectly in recovery so that she doesn't fall back into the jaws of compulsive gambling.

We can't submit a list of questions in recovery and have them answered so that we can refrain from making mistakes in our program. We have to take our recovery a step at a time. The answers are all there for us in recovery. But, part of the answer is working through the question.

I have a lot of questions.
I know my recovery program will lead me
through to the answers.

January 6

Honest differences are often a healthy sign of progress.

MAHATMA GANDHI

Everyone doesn't agree on everything. There is nothing wrong with that. Each person has their beliefs and opinions. They also have a background that determines why their beliefs are what they are.

In recovery, we can see this. It doesn't mean total agreement. What is does mean is we respect others' right to have their opinions. We don't have to be right or wrong. Neither do they. But, we do have to acknowledge their right to be heard and allowed to have their opinion.

~

I will respect others' opinions just as I respect my own.
I will allow them to have their opinion,
even if it doesn't agree with mine.

January 7

Speak while you are angry and you will make
the best speech you will ever regret.

AMBROSE PIERCE

Anger can bring out the worst in us. Words we wish we'd never said. Actions we wish we'd never taken. No one feels better in these situations, including us.

We do need to release our anger. But, we must look for productive ways in which to do so. Yelling and screaming never brings about a positive resolution.

The first thing we need to do is get out of the situation until we are in better control. Take a walk. Do some physical activity. Just get moving. This will give us time to think and decide what appropriate action to take.

~

I know that I have a right to be angry. How I deal with that anger, though, must also take others into account.

January 8

Once you have missed the first buttonhole,
you will have difficulty buttoning up.
ANONYMOUS

As recovering compulsive gamblers, we may have the tendency to want to skip a step or two. We may look at one of the twelve steps and think, "Yes, yes. I know what they're saying. I'll just go to the next step. I don't need to worry about this one."

We should remember that this step is the one we are working on. And we need to take each step at a time. To ensure that we thoroughly work through our program. To ensure that we continue to grow in recovery.

Missing a step in recovery is like missing the first buttonhole. Our recovery program won't "line up" like it should. We won't have the opportunity to identify our issues and deal with them. That means we can't expect to move forward in recovery.

~

I will work my program each step of the way.
I will not skip a step. I want to experience
all my growth in recovery.

January 9

Well begun is half done.

HORACE

How many times have we started something? If we look back into our compulsive gambling days, we will see many examples of this behavior. Start. Stop. Start. Stop. Over and over again, never completing anything.

Even in recovery, it is difficult to break this pattern. Maybe we are afraid of failure. Or, maybe we are afraid of success. Each one is likely. We know failure. We may not know much about success, however, and fear it just as much as failure.

What we begin, we need to keep working on. Like recovery. We have begun our program. Now, we need to continue in our growth.

~

I will work my program. I want to keep growing in the work I have begun.

January 10

Celebrate the moments of your life . . .
SLOGAN FROM A COMMERCIAL

How do you celebrate your life? Are you thankful for your life in recovery? Do you stop to look and the progress you've made? Do you congratulate yourself on your work in recovery? Do you recognize the steps you've taken?

It is important to realize that recovery is work. We're identifying years of negative behavior. And learning how to live a positive new life in serenity and peace.

So, pat yourself on the back. Do something nice for yourself. Take a bubble bath. Make time for that book you want to read. Go to the park. Ride your bike. Reward yourself.

I am working hard on my recovery.
I will take time to acknowledge my progress.
And reward myself.

January 11

January is a real downer for me. I struggle with real sadness and feel very depressed.

BARB

January is a tough month for Barb. Its right after the holidays. The holidays with her dysfunctional family are always a trial. Its cold in her home state, with snow and sub-zero temperatures. Its the month her husband left to move in with the woman he was having an affair with.

Barb recognizes that she has a difficult time during January. Singly, any of these reasons could cause a person to feel down. Added together, they can become more than a person could handle.

Barb doesn't deny her feelings about January. She acknowledges them and works with her support system to help her through her tough times. It doesn't mean she is wallowing in sadness or loneliness.

We all have times that are harder on us than others. What is important is that we identify our feelings and experience them. And that we seek the support of our friends and family.

I know that there are times I will feel sadness.
I will acknowledge my feelings and turn
to my support system for assistance.

January 12

Criticism, like rain, should be gentle enough
to nourish a person's growth without destroying their roots.

FRANK A. CLARK

As we grow in our recovery, we have the opportunity to assist others either on their own path or new to the recovery process. There are things that we have learned in recovery that have helped our growth. Others need to know that information, but we must make sure that we are doing our part to be supportive.

Recovery has shown us how fragile we are at times. So, in helping others, we must be aware that they may be fragile at this particular time. And the best help we can give them is to help them in a way that will help them grow. We don't want to squash their growth, we want to support it.

~

In helping others, I will remember
that a true friend in recovery is supportive.

January 13

Honesty, without compassion and understanding,
is not honesty, but subtle hostility.

DR. ROSE N. FRANZBLAU

As we continue in recovery, we find ourselves becoming honest for the first time in our lives. At times, we may feel the need to be brutally honest with others. What may happen is while we are secure in our belief that honesty is best, we use a method of displaying that honest that destroys the other person.

Honesty isn't about chewing people up and spitting them out. We need to look at the situation totally. Do we have all the information we need? Is there more about the person's background that we don't know? What really is causing this particular behavior or situation?

Even knowing these things, we still need to be compassionate. We've been where this person is now. Our self esteem was non-existent. It is ok to get our honest message out. We just need to be sure we are delivering that message so it has the greatest chance of success. For both ourselves and the other person.

~

I will not compromise my honesty.
However, I will make sure I look at the
whole situation before forming my message.

January 14

The best way out is always through.

ROBERT FROST

How many times have we tried to dodge our loneliness in recovery? We are so used to lots of activity and excitement around us that we have trouble being without those things. We don't know how to live without the excitement. We try to think up things we can do to make the pain go away, but it doesn't.

The first thing we need to do is admit our loneliness. It happens. The next thing we need to do is work through our loneliness. Is there a friend in recovery we can contact? Then, we need to make that first hard step and let them know we need some help.

We also learn that as we grow stronger in our personal recovery, the loneliness lessens. We learn to be comfortable with ourselves, something we have not done before. And we know what to do when that loneliness sets in. Our support system will be there for us in these times.

~

When loneliness comes, I am aware that this feeling is just temporary. I will reach out to my friends in recovery for assistance. I will work my program to become more comfortable with myself.

January 15

I gave up gambling. Now I am so bored,
it seems the only friend I have is the refrigerator.
CANDICE

Gambling took up a lot of our time. If we weren't in the casino or playing the pull tabs, we were thinking about gambling. Or we were scrambling to cover our losses.

Now that active gambling is absent from our lives, we may be looking for other distractions. Food may be one. We eat because we can't find another way to fill up our time. Every time we turn around, we're reaching for another donut, hamburger, ice cream or pizza.

As recovering gamblers, we need to be sure we aren't trading one addiction for another. Food can become a substitute for the loss of our gambling.

Sure, we have to eat to live. But, the next time we reach for another slice of pizza that we really aren't hungry for, stop and take a look at what is really going on. Are we hungry, or are we bored? Is there another, more positive activity we could be doing to fill our time? How about a walk? Reading to a child?

~

I know I have to eat to live. But, I will examine my habit to see if I am adding healthy activities into my life to replace the destruction of gambling.

January 16

There is nothing wrong with change, if it is in the right direction.
WINSTON CHURCHILL

As practicing gamblers, we were changing all the time. If we won, we were happy, generous; things were great. But, when our luck ran out, we could be angry and desperate. The main problem was we were constantly changing, according to our "wins."

In recovery, our lives are still changing. But they change a step at a time. No longer are we jumping from elation one day to desperation the next. We are working our program and learning to develop a life free of erratic changes. We're putting our lives on even ground.

~

My life is changing in the right direction.
Recovery makes that possible.

January 17

The real voyage of discovery consists not in seeking new lands but in seeing with new eyes.

MARCEL PROUST

While deep in our compulsive gambling, we saw the world through distorted eyes. We thought we were big shots if we won at gambling and terrible people if we didn't win.

Both versions of our beliefs were wrong. We can see that now in the new eyes we are looking through in recovery. Because recovery brings all the truths into focus. We are learning why we needed to gamble. We are also learning why we don't need to gamble.

I am thankful for my new eyes.
I see peace and happiness in the truths of recovery.

January 18

Admit your errors before someone else exaggerates them.

ANDREW V. MASON, M.D.

One of the most difficult things for us to do is admit our mistakes. As compulsive gamblers, we made many. In recovery, we will continue to make mistakes. After all, we are human and it is human nature to error at times.

What is different for us in recovery is our ability to look at ourselves and admit we have made and do make mistakes. We acknowledge our errors and stand ready to deal with the consequences. We don't make excuses. We don't blame others. We are responsible in our behavior. We are accountable.

I realize that I do make mistakes.
I will accept this and be accountable.

January 19

If you don't expose yourself to risk, you can't possibly learn anything.

GIFFORD PINCHOT

Safe. Secure. That's how we want to feel. For so long our lives have been surrounded with uncertainty and fear. We don't want to live being afraid of what in our past is following us, or what is ahead.

We can become so safe and secure that we don't grow. Because we become apprehensive about the steps we need to take to move forward in our process of recovery. What will happen if the outcome isn't the way we planned it? Will we get scared and run back to a life of compulsive gambling?

Life is about taking risks. But, we don't have to go it alone. We can use our support system to brace us as we move ahead in recovery. And we must remember that the process is ours, but the outcome isn't. If we have done our best with our process, then the outcome, no matter what it is, will never be a failure.

~

I will take appropriate chances with the
help of my recovery support system.
I will not worry about the outcome.
Instead, I will focus on my part in the process.

January 20

If you think you can do a thing,
or think you can't do a thing; you're right.
HENRY FORD

We decide what we can do. No one else can do that for us. If we continually tell ourselves that we are stupid, lazy and no good, we will believe that we are stupid, lazy and no good. And we will act out our belief in stupid, lazy, no good ways.

What we really need to do is affirm that we are good, smart, ambitious people. We have a lot to offer—ourselves and others. There are many things we do in our lives that are wonderful because we are wonderful human beings.

We have a choice—will we think of ourselves in a negative way? Or will we work to make our belief in ourselves stronger? When we have the chance to say or think something about ourselves, will we affirm ourselves in a positive way?

~

I will think of myself in positive, affirming ways.
I know that I am an extraordinary person.

January 21

The core of all this is personal boundaries. I don't think many of us are trained to have boundaries . . . to have rights . . . to recognize or respect others' boundaries.

LINDA MACK ROSS

One of the major things we learn in recovery is that we have the right to our personal boundaries. We get to define who we are and what is right for us. No one else in our lives—spouse, parents, children, boss, friends, neighbors, co-workers, pastor, or anyone else has the right to set our boundaries. That is our job.

The best approach is to start small. That's another thing we are not used to doing. Usually, we go for all or nothing. We need to define our boundaries and communicate those to others.

This can be done with respect and courtesy. And as we continue to stand firm with our boundaries, others can learn who we are. They may not agree with our personal boundaries. But, the fact is, they don't have to. They do, however, need to respect them.

~

I will reinforce my boundaries when it is appropriate to do so. It is not being disrespectful to others. It is being respectful to myself.

January 22

Learn the rules. Then break some.

H. JACKSON BROWN, JR.

Throughout life we've had others making the rules for us. Do this. Don't do that. Stand up straight. Get a job. On and on and on. We thought if we followed the rules, our family and friends would love us. They would want us. They would know we are valuable and worthy.

No matter how hard we tried to follow others' rules, we could never quite measure up. If we did one thing they requested, they'd either change the rules or add more. We ran the vicious cycle of doing more and more, yet pleasing others less and less.

We need to stop the cycle. Yes, we can acknowledge that others have rules which may be ok for them. That doesn't mean others' rules are right for us. We need to define what the rules are in our lives.

~

I will respectfully examine the rules others have for me.
I will decide, however, what is right for me.
I will not allow others to define my rules.

January 23

I find the great thing in this world is not so much where we stand,
as in what direction we are moving . . . . We must sail sometimes
with the wind and sometimes against but we must sail,
and not drift, nor lie at anchor.

OLIVER WENDELL HOLMES

Recovery isn't about standing still. Sure, it sometimes seems that for every step we take forward, there's more than one we're taking backwards. We think we have things under control, only to have something come apart. We'd like to just hide and stay away from life's problems.

Its important to keep moving. If we stand still, we can't grow. What happens when we stay in the same place is nothing. We may think nothing is harming us but, in reality, we are being harmed. Because we aren't moving ahead in our recovery process. We aren't strengthening our growth in serenity.

~

Today, I will move forward in recovery.
Even a baby step in the right direction
is a move forward.

January 24

Three times we went in. And three times we had to come out.

MEMBER OF RESCUE PARTY, L.A. EARTHQUAKE

Sometimes it seems like all the steps we take forward in recovery are just not getting us the results we think we should have. We want to be recovered! Yet, the bills keep coming; the phone keeps ringing and it seems like we, at times, cannot get a grip on our life.

Recovery doesn't promise us a problem-free life. It promises us the ability to deal with our problems. It helps us work through our frustrations and get on the path to serenity and peace. It allows us to deal with our problems and know that we are still worthy, responsible people.

Recovery shows us that we are strong. Unlike the unfortunate earthquake victims, in recovery we don't need rescuers. We admitted we were powerless over our gambling addiction. We pulled ourselves out of the flame of the terror of gambling. We rescued ourselves and continue to grow in recovery.

~

I will remember that recovery does not mean
I will never have issues in my life. Growth in recovery
teaches me that I can handle my problems.
And if I need help, it is available.

January 25

I get cabin fever in the cold, snowy winter.
After being indoors so long, I start to go crazy.

CHELSEA

One thing that recovering gamblers are not very good at is being alone with ourselves. This is not a negative for us, though. If we stop to think about it, we rarely have ever been alone. We typically found some distraction. That distraction for us was gambling.

Gambling was our friend. It gave us the highest highs we ever experienced. As long as we were winning, we felt like somebody. We were somebody. We had no end of "friends" to help us share in our winnings.

But, we also experienced the lowest lows we ever felt. Because gambling was also our enemy. When our luck ran out, our friends disappeared. We felt like nobody. We worried about money. We worried about our family and friends finding out what a loser we were. We thought if we could only score the "big win" everything would be all right.

We need to stop and realize that loneliness is normal in the early times of recovery. We're learning to identify our feelings. We're discovering who we are.

~

I know that loneliness will lessen as I grow in recovery.
I will use my support system to help me
be with others—and by myself.

January 26

There are admirable potentialities in every human being. Believe in your strength and your youth. Learn to repeat endlessly to yourself, "It all depends on me."

ANDRE GIDE

Confidence is not something most of us have a lot of. After years of hearing we weren't good enough, we can't do anything right, we make the wrong decisions, is it any wonder that our confidence is fragile?

In recovery, we learn to take a good look at ourselves. We discover who we really are. Blemishes and all. Beyond what we think we don't have, we find there are many wonderful qualities we do have. In each of us, there are many strengths and talents. Recovery allows us to find the confidence that's been lacking in our lives, and build on it.

~

I know that I have many strengths. Each day in recovery, I grow in the confidence that I am a wonderful, talented person.

January 27

There are two things people want more than sex and money . . .
recognition and praise.

MARY KAY ASH

We like to be acknowledged for our accomplishments. It feels good when others recognize the work we have gone through to get the job done. Throughout our lives we've hoped to have our efforts noticed by the people we love. Most times, though, it never happened.

Instead of praise, we got criticism. Not constructive criticism, but hard, cold, biting criticism about how we weren't good enough. How we would never amount to anything. How we could never measure up.

Is it a wonder that we struggle with raising our self esteem? How can we feel positive about ourselves when people we've cared about have told us we were losers?

It isn't easy at first. For every positive we feel about ourselves, we can think of ten negatives reasons we are inadequate. But, as we work our program and surround ourselves with people who do see the good in us, who do care, we learn the positives about who and what we are far outweigh the negatives.

~

I see the positives in me. I know I am
a wonderful person. I will refrain from using
negatives when looking at myself.

January 28

Nothing is interesting if you're not interested.

HELEN MACLNNES

During our compulsive gambling days, we had more excitement that we could handle. Some of it was positive, particularly when we were on a winning streak. But, most of it was negative excitement—the tenseness we felt when we couldn't pay the bills. Or when we called in sick again to miss work so we could go gambling. We weren't interested in anything but getting that big win.

In recovery, our interest in our program is directly related to our success in the program. We have to get involved, do the work, attend the meetings, associate with healthy people. By surrounding ourselves in the support of recovery, we know we can delight in the calm it has to offer.

~

I am interested in my recovery. I will stay involved in the process that assures me peace in my life.

January 29

If is seems like a struggle, I don't try to convince myself it isn't.
I acknowledge my feelings and move on.

TIM

Life, by itself, isn't always easy. When we add living with a gambling addiction, it is totally out of control. We cannot possibly manage our lives while actively gambling.

Life in recovery is not without struggles, either. We are entering new territory. The difference is two-fold: first, we are learning a lot about who we are; secondly, we experience our feelings. Most of us for the first time.

Recovery doesn't mean never having struggles. What it does mean is that we will have the ability to acknowledge our feelings and deal with them in the appropriate way.

~

I know I will have many feelings surface in recovery.
The important thing is to get in touch with my feelings.

January 30

Good thoughts not delivered mean squat.

KEN BLANCHARD

We usually mean well. We want to work our program. We think about how we want to act and make sure detailed plans are formed in our head. Then, it all just stays right there. In our head.

Because at times we do not act on our thoughts. We may decide it's too hard. Or it's too late. Or we're too tired. So our great plans never get put into action. That is how slips in our personal recovery program happen.

Recovery means taking the initiative to put our plans into action. Even when we are down. Even when the going seems a bit tough. We may not be able to do everything that we've planned. But, it is important to do something. Because each time we do, we have inched forward in our recovery. We don't need to take giant leaps; tiny steps will do just fine. After all, in a while, all those tiny steps will add up to a giant leap. And we can see how far we've come.

~

I will not leave my plans in my head. Today, I will act on my recovery plans to the best of my ability. I will move ahead.

January 31

They who feel guilty are afraid,
and they who are afraid somehow feel guilty."
ERIC HOFFER

Everyone wants to be liked. We want others to feel we are a good person, worth their friendship. The kind of person they would be happy to have in their lives. So, we try to do whatever others want us to so they will like us. Even though their requests become a burden to us, we wouldn't dream of ignoring them. It would make us feel guilty and unloved.

True friendship isn't about guilt, though. Friendship is a give and take situation.

Yet, we may be afraid of speaking up for ourselves because it may cost us a friendship. So, it is a vicious circle for us—we feel guilty because we are afraid to stick up for ourselves and we are afraid to move forward in our lives because we feel guilty for not wanting to pay the price for this demanding friendship.

Friends support friends. And, if we are in a relationship that is one-sided, it isn't a healthy relationship. Friendships are guilt-free.

~

I am a wonderful friend. I know I am worthy of a give and take relationship. I will feel no guilt.

February 1

There may be a responsible person, but there are no guilty ones.

ALBERT CAMUS

We have many responsibilities in our lives. Jobs. Family. Homes. Pets. School. Parents. But, while the list seems endless, the amount of time we have to spend is not. At times it can seem overwhelming to try to accomplish all the things that we feel we need to. We feel guilty when we just can't.

Who puts the guilt on us? Is it our spouse? Our kids? The boss? The School Administration? At times, maybe all of these. But, there is one person who really tends to be our harshest critic—ourselves. We feel we should be able to do all and everything. It is our responsibility. We want to please everyone.

In trying to please everyone, though, we really please no one. We aren't happy, so it isn't possible to make others happy. We are human. We are not responsible for everyone or everything that goes on in our world. We must learn to keep our responsibilities in perspective. We will do what we reasonably can. That is true responsibility. But we will not subject ourselves to guilt over the things we simply cannot do.

~

I will acknowledge the accomplishments I have made. I know I am a responsible person. I will be free of guilt over things I cannot control.

February 2

Life only demands from you the strength you possess.
Only one feat is possible—not to have run away.
DAG HAMMARSKJOLD

At times strength is hard to find. Our spouse may want us to do something. Our kids are begging for some of our time. The boss needs us to work additional hours. The neighbors need help. Our personal recovery program seems like it is in a maintenance mode, not moving ahead to our satisfaction.

It is during moments like this that we seem to be able to reach deep inside ourselves and pull out that last bit of strength we have. Then we find ourselves able to determine just what we can and cannot accomplish with others. We know our first priority is our program. Around that, we look at the other issues in our lives and use the strength to let others know what we are feeling. We allow ourselves to say yes to the things that need our attention and no to the things we are unable to satisfy.

Strength doesn't mean saying yes to everything. It means deciding what is possible. And feeling ok when it is not possible to do everything.

~

I have the strength to determine what is best in my life.
I will do what I feel I can and let others know, respectfully, what I cannot do. I will not feel guilty.

February 3

When a person lacks character, he is badly in need of a method.

ALBERT CAMUS

Our character is important. It is the definition of who we are. In the past others have determined what we should be—who we should be with, what we should do, how we should act, when we should speak. We have little or no control over our character. We believed, because of what we had been told and shown by others, that we were incapable of defining who we were. We were who others told us to be.

Thank goodness that has changed. In recovery, we have the opportunity to find out who we are. It is like the birth of a new person, a person who has been hidden away. It can be a bit scary meeting this person for the first time. But, as with all new friendships, our character will show itself in many ways as we grow in our personal recovery program. Therefore, we should treat this special person—ourselves—how we would treat any person important enough to us to be a significant part of our lives.

~

I realize that others have defined who I am in the past.
I am grateful to have this chance to find out
who I am in recovery.

February 4

If you act, you show character; if you sit still, you show it;
if you sleep, you show it.

EMERSON

Who we are is visible for the world to see. The actions we take tell a lot about who we are. What we are made of. The way we think things should be.

Looking at ourselves, we can discover a lot. Do our actions match the words we are speaking? Or are we saying one thing, while the behaviors we display show something completely different? This, too, says a lot about our character. How do we want our character displayed?

~

I want my character to show who I am.
I am a responsible, caring person.
My actions and words match each other.

February 5

Seeing the program work is what keeps me going.
I know my life is better.

PAT

Like many compulsive gamblers, Pat's life was out of control. Her marriage was failing. Her job was in jeopardy. Her family was distancing itself from her. Pat didn't feel she knew a lot. But, the main thing she did know was that life as she was living it was not working for her.

In recovery, Pat sees her work paying off. She experiences first hand the rewards of living a life not only free from gambling, but it also brings her in touch with the issues that have been haunting her all her life. She knows recovery works. As long as she works in recovery.

~

My program is important to my remaining free from gambling. I will work my program today and rejoice in its rewards.

February 6

Give your friend cause to blush, and you will be likely to lose him.

PUBLILIUS SYRUS

Humiliation is a feeling we are all too familiar with. Many of us have grown up with this feeling being a frequent visitor. Parents may have inflicted it on us in a number of ways. We were reminded over and over throughout our lives about how inadequate we were. Since we had no reason to believe otherwise, we believed we would never measure up to others' standards.

We know now that humiliation need not be a way of life for us. In fact, it does not have to be any part of our life. When others try to humiliate us, we have the strength to turn it back away from us in a respectful manner. We do not have to accept others' attempts to degrade us. We are strong in recovery.

~

I appreciate the strength I have to ward off humiliation.
It has no place in my life.

February 7

Came to believe that a Power greater than ourselves could restore us to a normal way of thinking and believing.

STEP 2

We can't do it alone. Luckily for us, we don't have to. We are fortunate to have a Higher Power with us on our road to recovery.

And with the guidance of our Higher Power, we are being restored to a normal way of thinking and believing. Thinking that we can be unencumbered by the chains of compulsive gambling. Believing that the true way of life is peace and serenity.

~

I treasure the presence of my Higher Power in my life.
I know I am not alone in my journey in recovery.

February 8

Man's loneliness is but his fear of life.
EUGENE O'NEILL

Loneliness is uncomfortable. We have not learned to be with ourselves. We are tense, distracted. We want someone around us.

But, no one can take away our loneliness. We need to work on this ourselves. There is much to do. Read a book. Write in our journal. Go see a movie. The point is to get comfortable with our new found friend—our "me" friend. Treat "me" the way we treat others we like. "Me" is just as important. And a good person to be with.

I will look inside myself for the answer to my loneliness.
I will become acquainted with me.

February 9

The lonely one offers his hand too quickly to whomever he encounters.

NIETZSCHE

Loneliness can be difficult to deal with. We don't know where to turn. We don't know what to do. Loneliness is an unfamiliar feeling to us.

But, is it really? During our days of gambling addiction, we had many people surrounding us. But, were we really involved with those people. Or did we just think we were. More likely, we were in the same location as others, but still very lonely in our addiction.

Loneliness can be overcome. It takes some effort. In the beginning, real strong effort to pull ourselves out. But it is well worth our attention.

~

I will work to combat my loneliness.
I know recovery means working through my loneliness.

February 10

No matter what the competition is,
I try to find a goal that day and better the goal.
BONNIE BLAIR

Goals are important in recovery. Today, a goal may be to contact that business we owe money to and arrange a repayment schedule. Or it may be to attend our support meeting. Each person's goals will be different and important.

Setting the goal is one step. Most importantly, though, is following through to complete that goal. If I don't arrange a repayment schedule, I have not met my goal. If I don't attend that support meeting, I may be taking a step backward in my recovery program.

I must be sure that setting my goals and then completing them go hand-in-hand. That is the way for me to succeed in my recovery program.

I will set my goals and work on them
to the best of my ability.

February 11

We are all worms, but I do believe I am a glowworm.
WINSTON CHURCHILL

Each person is unique in this world. We all have special gifts we bring. Jason is an outstanding architect. He has won many awards. Linda is a talented musician. Her concerts are sell outs and her recordings sell well. Both Jason and Linda bring wonderful gifts to this earth.

What they do with those gifts are just as important. Jason volunteers helping less privileged students work toward a high school degree. Sue teaches music to those not able to afford lessons. Each feels a responsibility to share their talents with others.

What is your talent? Can you sing well? Do you understand accounting? Can you simply read a wonderful story to a child? All these are important.

~

I will think about my talents. I am thankful for my gifts.
I will use them wisely.

February 12

Of course it's the same old story.
Truth usually is the same old story.
MARGARET THATCHER

Truth is important in recovery. We must be truthful with ourselves in looking at our issues and dealing with them. We must face our past and work our future always keeping the truth in the forefront.

Why is truth so important? Because if we are not truthful, if we don't own up to where we have been in our addiction and why we have been there, we can't hope to be able to move forward in recovery. If we continue to live an untruthful existence, our hope for the peace we seek in recovery will be dimmed.

Truth is the answer. Recovery without truth is not possible. Recovery with truth grants us the serenity we want.

~

I will be truthful to myself and my recovery.

February 13

I can never gamble again. Today.

AGNES

Taking on a lifetime of no gambling is overwhelming. How can I face the possibility of never gambling again? How can I get through thousands of days of keeping myself free from the woes of my gambling addiction?

We don't have to. What we do have to do is manage our recovery program today. Yesterday is behind us. Tomorrow hasn't appeared. When it does, we will deal with it then. But, for now, all we need concern ourselves with is today. And making today the best we can in recovery.

~

I will work my program today.
I know I may have many tomorrows.
I will deal with those as they come.

February 14

The course of true love never did run smooth.

SHAKESPEARE

Valentines Day is supposedly the day we show love for others. Bright red hearts are everywhere, expressing mountains of strong feelings for others.

Let's take this day to remember the most significant love of our lives. Ourselves. For too long we have been neglected. Everyone and everything else took first place. But, that's not the way it is anymore.

Reward yourself. Tell you how much you love yourself. Rejoice in your recovery and your newfound love.

I love me. And I am thankful
for this new person I have in my life
ME.

February 15

Being right half the time beats being half-right all the time.

MALCOLM S. FORBES

At times, we think we know what is right for others. We may give them advice about their recovery program without really thinking about their needs. We know what works for us and may think that all the move that we have made are right for others.

They may not be. While all the steps are the same for recovering compulsive gamblers, the process and pace in reaching those steps may vary somewhat. Each recovering individual deserves the opportunity to determine what will work best for them in their program. Respecting others' needs as well as our own means we really are working our program.

~

I am thankful for the progress I have made in recovery. I will remember that each person must work their own program.

February 16

Many are the varnish. Few are the wood.
JOSÉ NAROSKY

On the surface, gambling looks like the thing that can make life wonderful for us. In our illusion, it promises us the rich life, full of friends and material goods. We think we will have no worries.

We've been underneath the varnish of gambling. We've seen that there is no solid foundation to support us. Instead of riches, we got debt. The only friends we seemed to have were connected with gambling. When our luck was low, so was our circle of so-called friends. And material goods disappeared; houses and other possessions were lost to our addiction.

Recovery promises peace and serenity. Looking underneath the surface of these promises, we can see a sound foundation of truth and growth through living our program.

I will remember that many promises
look good on the surface. However,
few have the foundation of recovery.

February 17

Only your real friends will tell you when your face is dirty.
SICILIAN PROVERB

We need honesty in recovery. From ourselves and from the people we associate with. We may find in recovery that the people we are used to being with are not healthy for us. They may not understand recovery. They may be involved in their own compulsive gambling or other addiction. They may be angry at us for getting our lives together.

Real friends want what is best for us. We have determined that recovery is best for us. Surrounding ourselves with friends who are supportive in our efforts is what is best for us.

~

I know that I need to surround myself
with friends who support my recovery.
I am thankful for friends who aid me in this effort.

February 18

Happiness is a thing to be practiced, like the violin.
JOHN LUBBOCK

For years we lived in a world of much unhappiness. We may not have liked it, but it was familiar to us and, in an odd sort of way, comfortable. We knew what to expect. We knew we would not be happy.

Happiness is new to us. It's a joy. It's unfamiliar. It's uncomfortable. We don't know how to take it. We don't know what to do with it.

Enjoy it. Live in it. It may be uncomfortable now. Because it stretches our experiences. We don't think we deserve it. But, we do. And it will become a familiar friend to us. Just give it time.

I will enjoy the happiness I feel in recovery.
I am learning that I am deserving of such joy.

February 19

Only a fool tests the depth of the water with both feet.

AFRICAN PROVERB

Recovery shows us we have many possibilities. It can be so encouraging and we can be so in need of it that we jump in with both feet, soon to become overwhelmed by the work involved and the deliberate steps to be taken. We may become discouraged and give up.

But, working in recovery isn't about doing everything at once. It is about taking a step at a time. For some, maybe it is taking a half step. The important thing is to keep moving.

~

I will work my program a step at a time.
Real growth comes in reaching each milestone
having done the work required.

February 20

Why can't she see how much I'm going through?
Why can't she cooperate in my recovery?
PHIL

We are in a fulfilling recovery program. Others who are important in our lives may not be. They may not be able to really see the struggles we are going through. They may be uncomfortable with the changes they see in us. Before, even though they did not like our compulsive gambling, they knew our pattern of behaviors. They played their own role in our gambling addiction.

However, if they are not working their own recovery program, they will have difficulty dealing with ours. It isn't possible for them to work our program, they have to deal with the addiction process in their own lives.

We can't change others. We can only work our own program. But, we can acknowledge our own concern for their well-being. We can also hope they, in time, discover the wonder of recovery.

~

I hope my loved ones will work their own
recovery program. I wish the best for them,
but know I am only responsible for my own recovery.

February 21

If you begin to live life looking for the God
that is all around you, every moment becomes a prayer.
FRANK BIANCO

Came to believe that a Power greater than ourselves could restore us to a normal way of thinking and living. This second step in our recovery steps tells us we are not alone. We have someone stronger with us to help us in our freedom from gambling.

What we may not understand is that our Higher Power was always there for us. We just did not realize it. Or we chose to ignore it. All we need to do is to turn our lives over to our Higher Power, whomever that may be, and allow him/her to guide us in our recovery.

~

Living with my Higher Power in recovery means
I am not alone. I will seek guidance
from my Higher Power.

February 22

In every community, there is work to be done. In every nation, there are wounds to heal. In every heart, there is the power to do it.

MARIANNE WILLIAMSON

Recovery is a lot of work. Each day we can look back and see the steps of progress we have taken to reach where we are today. We can also look to this day to determine how we will work our program. Will we take another step forward? Or will this be a day we need to use our energy to maintain where we are at?

Either way, we need our heart to be in our program. For when we work with our heart in our program, we have the power to stay with the program. We have the strength to move forward in our process. We will continue to see the success of our work.

~

I will look inside to make sure I am
working my program with my heart in it.
I know I am growing in recovery.

February 23

Everybody works smarter when there's something in it for them.

MICHAEL LEBOEUF

There is something for every single person in recovery. Each person who commits to their personal recovery program will be rewarded with joy and peace. The truth is recovery works. Not just for some. Not just for those who say the right words. But, for everyone. Saying the right words isn't important. Working the total program words and actions is.

We take recovery a step at a time, experiencing all the lessons it has to offer. We accept that we need guidance in moving out of a life of compulsive gambling and into a life of peace.

~

I am committed to working my program. I seek the guidance of the program in releasing myself from the clutches of gambling, the gates of hell.

February 24

Brains, like hearts, go where they are appreciated.

ROBERT MCNAMARA

Our minds are mysterious wonders. If we constantly think negative thoughts, we will live in the negative world we have created for ourselves. If we think positive thoughts, our world will be more positive. It isn't hard to choose which one we would prefer.

We want a positive world. However, we know more about the negative world. As we learn to create a positive world for ourselves, we find that it is awkward for us. We don't know this world, we don't know how to live in it.

Recovery teaches us how to release the negative thoughts from our lives and let the positive thoughts enter. As we take steps in our new, positive world, we know it will become familiar to us. We know we do not want to return to the old world we knew so well.

I want to live my life positively.
I will find positive things in my life
and rejoice in their pleasure.

February 25

One can be bored until boredom
becomes the most sublime of all emotions.
LOGAN PEARSALL SMITH

If we allow our boredom to overtake us, it will become a normal behavior for us. We will no longer seek to turn that boredom into something more productive for us. We will consider it a part of us. We may not like it, but it will help define who we are.

Instead of a boredom liver, we need to be a boredom reliever. Do we really want boredom to become a regular? If not, we have many opportunities to turn our boredom around. If we look around us, there are all sorts of things to do, places to go, people to see. And if none of these interest us, it is the perfect time for us to just spend some time with ourselves. To get to know who we are. To become comfortable just being with us.

I do not want boredom to become part of my life.
I will search for ways to eliminate it.

February 26

Man is the only animal that can be bored.

BYRON

When we think about it, animals never appear to be bored. When they are not sleeping, they are playing or hunting or searching. Their interest in life seems to be unending. Life is never dull for them.

To be fair, though, most animals don't face the same challenges that we humans do. They have us to care for them. But, we can learn something from them about boredom. When it seems like we can't find anything to relieve our boredom, we should take a lesson from animals. There is always something new to explore. When is the last time you took the kids to the playground? Have you visited the library recently? How about volunteer work? We don't have to be bored—there is plenty to keep us involved.

~

I will look for things to do when I feel boredom coming on. I know there are many things I can do. I just need to try.

February 27

I thought I knew it all. I could recite the twelve steps by heart."

NATASHA

We are so engrossed in the promises that recovery offers, that we plunge right in and try to learn everything. We read every book on the subject. We become authorities on the subject of compulsive gambling and how to recover from it.

However, our actions are different from our words. We talk a good show, but we don't act on our words. We can recite every step, but we aren't living them. Talking about recovery is important. But, living and working our recovery program is essential.

~

I am careful to ensure my actions in my
personal recovery program match my words.
I work my program the way I should.

February 28

Passions are less mischievous than boredom,
for passions tend to diminish, boredom to increase.
JULES BARBEY D'AUREVILLY

While we were actively gambling, our lives were filled with much excitement. If we gambled in a casino, bingo or pull tab establishment, there was a lot of activity surrounding us. Lights, people, noise all around. Outside of our chosen gambling establishment, we still met excitement, although much more negative. There was always the anxiety encompassing our lives. Bill collectors calling. Families complaining.

Now that we have removed ourselves from these situations, we may find ourselves bored. The continuous excitement and activity is gone. We feel the withdrawal and don't know how to fill our lives. Boredom can have us itching for something to do.

We must ensure that something is healthy for us. We cannot let boredom send us into situations which will undermine the progress we have made in recovery. Recovery is important to us. Therefore, we need to establish emergency plans for those times when boredom threatens to harm us.

~

I will make sure I have activities identified
for times I feel boredom creeping in.

February 29

Gambling was agony. I was in pain all the time.

BUD

Like many of us, Adam thought that if he just made that "big win" the pain would go away. He would be able to pay back all his debts. He would be able to spend more time with his wife and kids. He would be able to focus more attention on his job.

Also like many of us, Adam never got that big win. He sure tried. Over and over again. Spending more money. Breaking more promises. Telling more lies.

Gambling and pain go hand-in-hand. Recovery takes us through our pain and beyond, allowing us to experience the relief from the painful memories of compulsive gambling.

I am thankful for the process of recovery.
I am relieved from the pain of compulsive gambling.

March 1

To believe with certainty we must begin with doubting.
STANISLAUS I OF POLAND

We doubted that gambling was the life we wanted to lead. Yet, we did not know how to free ourselves from this grip of vicious problems. We knew our lives were out of control. We could not get away from gambling, but we knew we could not go on with our gambling addiction.

In recovery, we came to believe that we could release ourselves from the control of compulsive gambling. As we work our program, we know we are becoming stronger in removing ourselves from the danger that compulsive gambling holds for us. Believing in recovery is important to working our own program.

~

I no longer doubt the rewards
that recovery offered. I receive the benefits
of my personal recovery program.

March 2

He does not believe that does not live according to his belief.

THOMAS FULLER

If we say that we believe in victory from gambling, yet live in a manner that does not reflect that, we are really showing that we do not believe in recovery. To believe that we can refrain from actively gambling means that we have to live our personal recovery program. Recovery is meant to change our lives. For the better. But, we must do our part to ensure that change is made for ourselves. We must make the commitment to live our lives in a manner that will bring a positive impact for us in recovery.

Walking our beliefs proves to ourselves that we do believe in the peace and serenity that recovery has to offer us. It can show others that we are serious about our personal recovery program. More important, though, it reinforces to us in recovery our goals of freedom from compulsive gambling.

~

I believe in my personal recovery program.
I will live my life according to my beliefs.

March 3

Everything possible to be believed is an image of truth.

WILLIAM BLAKE

Belief in recovery is an important step in our personal program. If we believe that a recovery program can set us free from the problems of compulsive gambling, we can start to live the truths recovery has to offer. Recovery is not an elusive goal that we have waved in front of our faces, only to have it pulled away at the last minute. Recovery is backed by truth. It is proven by many people who have participated in their own personal recovery program and have found the achievement of freedom from gambling that recovery promises.

Truth is important to our recovery. If we believe in the truths of recovery, we can allow ourselves to follow the steps necessary to ensure our liberty from gambling continues.

~

I believe in the truths of recovery.
I will work my program today
knowing I shall remain free from gambling.

March 4

When you want to believe in something you also have to believe in everything that's necessary for believing in it.

UGO BETTI

To believe in recovery is to believe the process that takes us on this journey. We can't believe in the concept of recovery, yet neglect to participate in the process required. If we want recovery, we have to take the steps necessary to move us along on our personal journey. The pace we set for ourselves isn't as important as ensuring that we stay on the path that is showing us the way to peace in our lives.

Recovery requires us to work our program. To become involved in our personal recovery every step of the way. We can't participate in something in which we don't believe. But, if we believe, it is important for us to involve ourselves fully, so that we can reap all of the benefits recovery has to offer.

~

I believe in my personal recovery program.
I know that the process is important
to finding success in recovery.

March 5

If you think in terms of failure, I can guarantee you failure.

ELAINE

Our mind has great control over our actions. For years we have been told that we did not deserve a life of happiness. Others have been critical of our lives. We felt we were stupid. We felt that no matter what we did, it was not good enough. Because of this, we held ourselves back from trying new things. The result would be the same as always; we would fail.

It doesn't have to be this way. In recovery, we learn that we do deserve a life of happiness. We learn to defeat the negative images in our mind and replace them with positive images. We learn to turn our thinking around so we can prove to ourselves we are not failures. We are successful—in recovery.

I will think in positive terms today.
I will not let negative thoughts enter into my mind.

March 6

It seems I'm always learning. When will I know?

JOANNE

At first in recovery, we have much to learn. We are trying to rid ourselves of old behaviors and move forward in our recovery program. New behaviors seem strange to us. We feel awkward, out of place.

It is important for us to stay with these new behaviors. After a while, they will become familiar to us. We will be able to act in ways which promote our healthy recovery without even thinking about it. Positive behaviors will be spontaneous for us.

I will continue to work on the new
behaviors that I am learning in recovery.
They are becoming more comfortable to me.

March 7

The conduct of our lives is the true mirror of our doctrine.

MONTAIGNE

Bill says he believes in his personal recovery program. Yet, every Friday, Bill rides along with his buddies to the casino. He says it is to maintain his friendships and he just goes for the buffet and show. He hasn't yet gambled, but admits it is not easy refraining when the temptation is so near.

Working a personal recovery program means removing ourselves from situations where we may slip. While it is understandable that Bill wants to maintain his friendships, he has to realize that it may be at the expense of his own recovery. Bill needs to remove himself from situations and friends that do not support his recovery.

We also need to ensure that the situations that we place ourselves in support our recovery process. Our friendships also need to reinforce our need for freedom from gambling. What we rub up against rubs off.

~

I will keep myself free from situations
which may undermine my recovery process.
I will surround myself with friends
who support my goals.

March 8

Behavior is a mirror in which everyone displays his own image.

GOETHE

When we look in the mirror, we can see a number of things, depending on what age we are. Older people may see wrinkles around the eyes and a little graying of the hair. Teens may agonize over acne on their face or braces in their mouth. We all see things about our personal appearance in the mirror that we like and dislike.

Our behavior is also a mirror for us. It is a direct reflection on how we feel. It shows what our intentions are towards living our lives. It displays the response we have to working our personal program.

What does your mirror say about you? Are you working your recovery program? Does your behavior reflect this? Or does it reflect that you are talking about recovery, yet not acting in a way that will lead you towards the peace and happiness you want?

~

My behavior is an example of how I feel.
I will make sure my behavior leads me
forward in my personal recovery program.

March 9

Carrying around this guilt has weighed me down.

ARNIE

We enter recovery with an enormous amount of guilt over the lives we have been leading while actively gambling. We know a lot of the harm we have caused. We also know we have blocked out some of the problems we have been involved with. It seems like we have really messed up.

We learn in recovery to deal with that guilt. Guilt didn't start with our compulsive gambling. It started way before that, in our childhood. Guilt is one of the things that leads us to our addiction. If we grow up always feeling guilty about something, it is hard to imagine a life free from guilt.

But, life can be free from guilt. In recovery we identify the causes of guilt and work through how to let go of it. We can look at our behavior and separate the actions from the guilt. Both need our attention. An both will get it in recovery.

~

My guilt stems from issues before I began
my compulsive gambling. I am happy to
be able to work through my guilt and let it go.

March 10

A beautiful behavior is better than a beautiful form; it gives a higher pleasure than statues or pictures; it is the finest of the fine arts.

EMERSON

We can ask ourselves if our behavior matches the goals we set for ourselves in recovery. Do we say we want serenity, yet behave in ways which contradicts this? If so, we cannot possibly meet the milestones we hope to.

The manner in which we conduct our personal recovery plan says a lot about our real intentions for recovery. We need to make sure that the verbal and behavioral messages we are sending match. It is easy to say what we want. It is more difficult to follow through on those words. But, it is necessary for the success of our personal recovery.

~

I will monitor my behavior. I want my behavior to reflect the goals I have set for myself in recovery.

March 11

He who begins many things finishes but few.

ITALIAN PROVERB

Commitment is difficult for us. Our intentions are good. However, over and over again we find ourselves unable or unwilling to follow through on the commitments we have made. We continue to begin new promises only to fail to fulfill them. In the process we have hurt many, including ourselves.

Our commitment is vital to our personal recovery program. Without our ongoing involvement, we cannot hope to grow in the peace recovery offers us. We need to hang in with our program, even when the going gets rough. Even when we feel bored. Even when we are scared.

By remaining strong in our commitment to recovery, we know we can find the happiness we deserve. The follow through we display will reward us with the serenity we want.

~

I am committed to working
my personal recovery program.

March 12

A hard beginning maketh a good ending.

JOHN HEYWOOD

Beginning our personal recovery program can seem difficult. We have been struggling for a long time while actively gambling. We are looking for relief from the problems we had. But, we don't know if we have the ability to put out any more energy.

The good thing about beginning recovery is that we can take it a step at a time. Little by little, we begin to regain our strength. As we see the progress we have made, we find renewed energy that will continue to carry us through on our journey to peace.

~

I need only move a step at a time in recovery.
I am grateful for the energy
I have to work on my program.

March 13

The eye of the master fattens the steed.

SPANISH PROVERB

How we look at things has a lot to do with the outcome. If our attitude is the world is against us, we will live as a victim, always blaming others. If, on the other hand, we feel we can accomplish anything we want to, our attitude will lead us to a more fulfilling life.

In recovery, the attitude we bring to the program is vitally important. If we decide that we want to work our program, knowing the outcome is peace, we will be successful in our recovery. If, on the other hand, we are involved in recovery because we are forced to and we don't believe it can help us, we will be unsuccessful in our attempts to find peace in our lives.

~

I will ensure my attitude reflects positively towards my personal recovery process.

March 14

If you look at life one way, there is always cause for alarm.

ELIZABETH BOWEN

Our attitude is important in the way we work our program. if we go into recovery thinking all we have to do is show up, the chances of us finding serenity are nonexistent. If we have a chip on our shoulder and think that others in recovery are different from us, we cannot hope to find support for our recovery.

Beyond showing up, we need to participate in our personal recovery process. We need to dig in and work our program. We need to knock that chip off our shoulder and build our support system around us.

Attitude is key to our recovery. If we keep our attitude healthy, the efforts we put into our program will lead us to the serenity we seek.

~

My attitude is key to my recovery.
I will make sure my attitude reflects
my involvement in my program.

March 15

Lean too much upon the approval of people,
and it becomes a bed of thorns.

TEHYI HSIEH

We have people in our lives whom we want to please. It could be our parents, who may have continually told us we were bad. It could be our spouse, whom we have hurt. It could be our supervisor, who appraises our work performance. All around us are people from whom we seek approval.

We can never please everyone, though. What might please our parents may displease our spouse. What could please our supervisor may anger our children. And on and on it goes.

The only person we can really please is ourselves. If we are working our program to the best of our ability, we know we cannot count on the approval of others. The person we truly need approval from is us. We learn in recovery how to find peace and happiness. We only have responsibility for ourselves.

~

I will not seek approval from others.
I know I am a capable, loving individual.
I approve of me.

March 16

The math is simple; one person plus one recovery program equals one success.

LARRY

One plus one does not always equal two. Larry, an experienced accountant, knows this first hand. Larry will tell you that compulsive gambling was driving his life out of control. When he was confronted with his stealing funds from his employer to cover gambling losses, Larry knew that stealing plus gambling did not lead to a happy life.

Larry feels his recovery program is an equation he can identify with. "If I work my program, really involving myself in my recovery, it leads me forward. No more fear of being discovered. No more tension over covering gambling losses. With my growth, I am once again earning the trust of those who I have harmed. It may take time. In fact, some may not feel able to trust me totally again. But, I know my work and my process in recovery will equal success in a life free from gambling."

~

Freedom from gambling allows me to live a life in serenity.
I am successful in the recovery work I do.

March 17

Anxiety and conscience are a powerful pair of dynamos.

ARNOLD J. TOYNEBEE

Anxiety can be scary for us, even in recovery. When it comes into our lives, it can paralyze us from progressing in our personal recovery program. We don't know what to do or how to act.

It doesn't have to immobilize us, though. When anxiety strikes, we must call on our support system to assist us in moving through this time. Working with our support system can give us the guidance we need to release our anxiety.

I will call for support in dealing with my anxiety.
I will not be paralyzed by fear.

March 18

Do what you are good at! Stop worrying about the things you can't do.
Do the things you can—even better!

COVERT BAILEY

Each of us is good at doing many things. Too often, though, we focus on things others do well and wish we could be like them. Maybe we know someone who is a talented artist. Or another person who is a computer whiz. We can be thankful we do know people like them.

We enrich others' lives, too. Perhaps we can't paint a masterpiece, but we can color a drawing with a child, knowing it makes that child feel very special. Maybe we can't design a complicated computer system, but we could be the only person around who is an expert at fixing a neighbor's car.

We have many talents. And it is up to us not to look at what we cannot do. Instead, we need to make sure we do our very best at what we can do well.

I will remember that I have many talents.
I will put my best foot forward and not worry
if others have talents I don't.

March 19

Having made an effort to practice these principles in all our affairs, we tried to carry this message to other compulsive gamblers.

STEP 12

If we are new to our recovery, yet have experienced some of the joy of recovery, we may be too anxious to help others. The fact is, we can only give what we, ourselves, have got.

If we have reached step 12, we are continuously living our program. Walking our talk. We are experiencing stability, joy, and serenity in our lives.

This we can share. We can help others new to recovery. We can be there for them. Make a phone call of encouragement. Visit those who need it. Tell our story.

~

I will share the life I have gained in recovery with others.
I know they must do their own work,
but I will help spread the joy of recovery.

March 20

How can I work my program when I am so focused on my anger?

JEFF

Steve's boss did something that made him so angry that Steve couldn't forget it. Even though Steve and his boss discussed the issue, Steve was still upset about it long after the work day had ended. It was the last thing Steve thought about that night. It was on his mind the first thing the next morning.

Steve couldn't do any more with his boss to resolve this issue, but Steve knows he had to address his anger. How, though? In this case, by writing a letter to his boss, stating Steve's point of view on the issue, and his feelings.

Certain grounds for firing Steve, you think? Maybe. But Steve didn't mail the letter. He only wrote it. Then, Steve tore it up.

The important thing for Steve is that he released his anger in a constructive manner.

~

I will take action to release my anger.
I will remember to Let Go and Let God.

March 21

When I think of giving up, the program reminds me to give up that kind of stinking thinking.

SUZETTE

We all have thoughts of giving up. Recovery is not the life we are familiar with. Active gambling is. So, in our journey to discover the life we can give ourselves in recovery, we are moving through territory that is unfamiliar to us. Territory that includes dealing with issues, identifying feelings and confronting behaviors that led us to an unhealthy lifestyle.

When we feel like giving up and returning to our life of gambling, what we need to turn to immediately is our program. Recovery has the answers we seek in our lives. If we take this moment to "give up" our thought of quitting, we find a happier, peaceful existence in recovery.

~

When I feel like giving up, I will turn to my program to find the answers I seek.

March 22

Boundary, n. In political geography, an imaginary line between two nations, separating the imaginary rights of one from the imaginary rights of the other.

AMBROSE PIERCE

Deb's boss reprimanded her in front of others. At first, Deb was going to let it pass until she and her boss could discuss the issue privately. But, her boss started saying things that were clearly untrue. To not speak up could leave the impression to the others that Deb was not doing her job.

When her boss stopped talking, Deb respectfully spoke up. Without attacking her boss verbally, she set the record straight. Deb used statements like "I did check the hotels for the proper meeting room." "I did go to the hotel early to make sure everything was set up correctly." And so on.

By responding in this manner, Deb did three things: she took responsibility for her specific actions; she did not let her boss overstep Deb's boundaries; and, most importantly, Deb felt a sense of relief and freedom from momentary abuse, knowing that it is ok to respectfully stick up for herself.

~

I will remember that it is my right to stand up for what is right. I will respectfully not let others create boundary issues for me.

March 23

There is no fury like that against one who we fear, may succeed in making us disloyal to beliefs we hold with passion, but have not really won.

LEARNED HAND

Zachary asked his Aunt Ann to open the sun roof on her car. Normally, she'd say yes, but it was winter and people don't open sun roofs in winter.

Aunt Ann thought to herself, "Says who?" They both had warm coats, hats and mittens on. They could turn the heat way up and open the sun roof for a short distance on a clear day. So they did—and laughed all the way. It was harmless and fun.

Aunt Ann first said no because her mind immediately kicked in to others' messages. She had been living according to what others told her for so long, that she works now on remembering what's right for her.

~

I will live by my beliefs. I will not harm others, but I will also not let others dictate my life.

March 24

There can be no friendship without confidence,
and no confidence without integrity.
SAMUEL JOHNSON

Throughout our lives, we have had many people we though were friends. But some of those friendships may have been based on unhealthy behaviors. We may have acted in certain ways in order to be accepted by our friends.

Real friendships are based on respect and caring for one another. Real friends allow others to be themselves and are considerate of healthy boundaries their friends have established.

Today, I will examine my relationships
with my friends. I will surround myself
with healthy, mutually respectful friendships.

March 25

Things which matter most must never be
at the mercy of things which matter least.
GOETHE

Abstinence is important to our recovery process. So we must take whatever actions necessary to ensure our abstinence from compulsive gambling.

That may mean we need to take a look at our relationships. Who are the people we used to spend our time gambling with? Are they still a big part of our life? Are they supporting our recovery? Or do they attempt to sabotage it?

~

Today I will look at the relationships I am in.
I will ask myself if these relationships
are healthy for my recovery program.

March 26

What lies behind us and what lies before us
are tiny matters compared to what lies within us.
OLIVER WENDELL HOLMES

What are our values? What is important to us? For so long, others have told us what our values are. Even if we did not feel good about those values defined for us by others, we went along with them.

That was before beginning our recovery program. In our program, we are defining our values for ourselves. We know what is important to us. And we are learning how to set limits and boundaries based on our values.

~

I will define my values for myself.
They are right for me. Therefore,
no one can tell me they are wrong.

March 27

The significant problems we face cannot be solved at the same level of thinking we were at when we created them.

ALBERT EINSTEIN

When we were gambling, we tired to solve our problems with more gambling. But, it didn't work. We couldn't solve our addiction while we actively practiced it.

Thank goodness those days are over. And, they will stay behind us as long as we practice our new life—the life of clean living.

Because now we're at a new level of thinking. No more stinkin' thinkin' for us.

I am thankful to be on a new level of thinking.
A level of serenity.

March 28

Because she is so capable, so multifaceted, so talented, she is expected to be all things to all people. Nobody can do that.

SALLY QUINN

Living up to others' expectations. We tried doing that for years. Letting others define us doesn't work for us.

It robs us of our feelings. It cheats us of our thoughts. It abuses us.

Thank goodness we're through living our lives for others. They have their own lives to live. This one belongs to us. To live the way that is best—for us.

I will remember that I am the one who defines my life. This is my life to live.

March 29

Deep down inside I wanted to say it the way
I was thinking it. So . . . help me, God.
PRESIDENT BILL CLINTON

Everyone needs the help of their Higher Power. The President does. We do. We cannot do it alone.

We don't need to. Help is ours for the asking. The key is asking. Knowing that we need our Higher Power involved in our recovery.

We tried it without our Higher Power. We know that never worked. But, working with our Higher Power ensures us the peace and serenity we need.

~

My Higher Power is there for me.
To help me in my recovery.

March 30

Reliving the pain when meeting someone entering recovery reminds me I never want to experience it first hand again.

RYAN

Besides earning our empathy, newcomers to the recovery process bring a lot of visible pain. It is easy to identify their pain because it practically enters the room before them, shouting out loud and clear. They don't know how they are ever going to get a better life. They don't understand recovery. They only know that life hurts.

We know that pain first hand. Being in the program longer than a newcomer, we also know that recovery is far better than the pain and hurt we felt while actively gambling. We know the recovery process is work, but the rewards far outweigh the effort we put into our program.

~

I am thankful for my freedom from the pain of gambling. I will remember I do not want to experience that pain again.

March 31

All growth is a leap in the dark, a spontaneous, unpremeditated act without benefit of experience.

HENRY MILLER

Seven years ago Jane reached a crisis point—her personal bottom. She started her recovery work.

Jane's been working her program ever since. Every day. A model recovering gambler? Jane would be the first to say NO. She's had frustrations, tears, anger, fear.

But what is amazing to Jane is how she has grown in those seven years and who she's become. "I remember saying when I hit bottom that I was afraid to find out who I was because I might not like me," she says.

But, Jane didn't like who she was before recovery. So, she could only go up. "Surprisingly, when I look back, I have come a long way," Jane reflects, "One day at a time."

~

I know I'll work my program the rest of my life—
day by day. Today I will take time
to reflect on my progress.

April 1

You're not free until you've been made captive by supreme belief.

MARIANNE MOORE

All during her childhood, Sue was told that she couldn't do athletic things. She was taller and heavier than other kids until junior high school Although Sue was never fat, she grew up with the image of herself as fat, ugly and not able to do anything athletic.

After working her recovery program for a while, Sue started to feel better about herself. She'd always been interested in golf, but never tried it because of the childhood messages.

Sue tried it. And with practice, found she was pretty good at golf.

What other messages are ingrained in us? What are we wanting to try but have been holding back on because of what others told us?

~

I recognize that some of the definitions
of my life were placed on me by others.
I will decide what is right for me.

April 2

I'm angry. All the time. It scares me.

MARI

Anger can be healthy. It can also be self-destructive if we do not learn to deal with it effectively. Recovery does not mean we can never get angry at anyone or anything. What it does mean is that we have to deal with it in an appropriate manner.

Mari obviously has not learned to deal with her anger. She is angry all the time. That is a red flag that says she has identified her anger, but has not come to terms with the issues that cause it. In order for Mari to move on in her program, she must first work through her anger. Identify it, work through it and then let it go.

I will take the time to identify the cause of my anger. I will work through my issues and release the anger I feel.

April 3

For people who live on expectations, to face up to their realization is something of an ordeal

ELISABETH BOWEN

Sometimes we're just plain tired. We may have tried to cram too much living into too little day. We had to work, parent and take care of our home responsibilities.

Because of this, we may be irritable. We may snap at our child for child-like behavior, expecting him or her to know what we need—quiet and rest.

We must be careful about projecting our feelings onto our children. We were in their shoes once. How did it feel to us? Were we allowed to be child-like, just like children should?

~

I will remember that my expectations
of my children are to be children.
not miniature adults. At the same time,
I will remember I need nurturing, too.
And make sure I get it.

April 4

In every work a reward added makes the pleasure twice as great.

EURIPIDES

Take five minutes. Think about all the positive things about working your recovery program. Go look in the mirror. Tell yourself one of those positive things.

Then reach over your shoulder and give yourself a pat on the back. Have a nice day!

~

Today, I will remember the importance of rewarding myself. Some of my victories may seem small, but they are victories all the same. I'm doing a good job!

April 5

Life used to be grandiose. Now it's just grand.

WADE

In recovery, we talk a lot about character flaws. One we have identified is our ability to be quite grandiose in our behavior. We know the answers to everything. We were big shots while we were gambling. At times, we may still act out that behavior, even though we are in recovery.

In a world of peace and serenity, there is no room for grandiosity. It adds nothing to our recovery process. In fact, it can set us way back in the progress we are working so hard to achieve. It is up to each of us to first identify the times we are exhibiting this behavior. Second, we have to actively work on removing it from our lives.

~

I will refrain from acting on any impulse I have
to behave with grandiosity. I want my live
to be free from this type of behavior.

April 6

We admitted we were powerless over gambling—
that our lives had become unmanageable.

STEP I

We can't do it alone. Luckily for us, we don't have to. We are fortunate to have a Higher Power with us on our road to recovery.

And with the guidance of our Higher Power, we are being restored to a normal way of thinking and believing. Thinking that we can be unencumbered by the chains of compulsive gambling. Believing that the true way of life is peace and serenity.

~

I treasure the presence of my Higher Power in my life.
I know I am not alone in my journey in recovery.

April 7

Individualism is rather like innocence;
there must be something unconscious about it.
LOUIS KRONENBERGER

How would I describe myself? How would I tell another person about me?

Does this make me uncomfortable? You bet it does. After all, we've spent most of our lives not knowing who we are. And diverting attention away from ourselves.

Not anymore. Sure, we may be awkward at first. But, in taking a good look at ourselves in recovery, we can be proud to meet that person we never knew existed. That wonderful new friend we've found.

~

Today I will think of five positive words
to describe my new friend—me. I will look myself
in the mirror and tell myself those words—out loud.

April 8

If you count every step, you will make a long journey of it.
THOMAS FULLER, M.D.

There's a saying that we must be careful of the camel who slips his nose under the tent. That's because he'll continue to inch his way in until we find the camel in the tent!

We can use this thought in two ways. One could be a warning to us to watch out for unhealthy behaviors sneaking back into our lives until we are once again in the grips of compulsive gambling.

On a more positive note, though, we can use this thought to remind us that working our program inches us further along in our recovery process. And further away from unhealthy behavior.

~

Like the camel, I choose to positively inch
my way in my program, advancing
in healthy behaviors all the way.

April 9

Our entire life, with our fine moral code and our precious freedom, consists ultimately in accepting ourselves as we are.

JEAN ANOUILH

Sometimes we just have nothing to say. It's ok Accept it. It's part of who we are.

There are a number of other things we can accept about ourselves, too. They are different for each of us. They are a part of who we are.

And who we are is beautiful.

~

I know that there are times I need some quiet time.
For myself. I will take care of me.

April 10

It is not enough to take steps which may some day lead to a goal;
each step must be itself a goal and a step likewise.

GOETHE

Sometimes things seem formidable. Take this daily reader, for instance. The authors knew that they needed to write 366 pages to complete the book. How would they ever be able to come up with 366 inspirational thoughts?

One message at a time. You see, 366 messages seemed like a mountain they wouldn't be able to climb. But, they knew they could write one message. Then one more. And another. Until one day there were 366 messages.

That's how our recovery program works. One day at a time. It's hard to comprehend forever without gambling. But, we can make it one day. Today. Tomorrow's another day. We'll make that day, too. Tomorrow. For now, though, we'll take care of today. Only today.

~

I will not let forever get in the way of working
my program I will work it today. One day at a time.

April 11

I called out for help. Thank goodness someone heard me.

REGINA

Calls for help come in many ways. Some are able to simply say, "I need help." Others show signs of poor choices or erratic behavior. Someone else may attempt suicide. All are calls for help.

Each one of us called for help in our own way. Lucky for us, someone heard our call. Because of this, we were led into our personal recovery program. We were shown a program that would free us from our addiction of compulsive gambling. We were shown a program that promises us peace and serenity.

~

I am thankful someone heard my call for help.
I am thankful for recovery.

April 12

However much thou art read in theory,
if thou hast no practice thou art ignorant.

SXDI

People spend a lot of money on golf. They want to get just the right clubs so they can hit the perfect drive.

No matter how much money a person spends, they won't get better if they don't practice swinging that club over and over again. Then, one day, they do hit a great drive off the tee, straight and far.

In our recovery program we practice freedom from compulsive gambling each day. Over and over again. It's the way we stay on the straight line of tranquility.

~

I am practicing my freedom from gambling daily.
One day at a time.

April 13

I was desperate for a win. I was desperate for a loss. I was desperate.

GENE

Desperation was constant when we were actively involved in gambling. We wanted so badly to win so we could clean up everything in our lives. We wanted to lose so we could, hopefully, escape the reminders of our inability to free ourselves from this addiction.

We finally found our escape. We entered our personal recovery program. Our desperation led us into the loving arms of recovery, where we found a life free from this hopeless feeling. As long as we continue to work our program, freedom from desperation is guaranteed. We have to quit to win!

~

In recovery, I live a life free from desperation.
I rejoice in my release from this painful feeling.

April 14

Peace is liberty in tranquility.

CICERO

Coming back. Those two words used to mean we were behind money-wise in our gambling and were, therefore, gambling again to try to recoup our losses.

It has a new meaning to us in recovery. Here, coming back means we are working our program. We are living clean. We are reclaiming our lives. We are coming back over and over again to the healthy behaviors of recovery.

I am coming back.
To a life of serenity.
To a life of joy.

April 15

Space flights are merely an escape, a fleeing away from oneself, because it is easier to go to Mars or to the moon than it is to penetrate one's own being.

CARL JUNG

In Minnesota one of the biggest winter sports is ice fishing. Once the lakes freeze, hundreds of hearty Minnesotans bundle up and head out.

After drilling a hole in the thick ice, fishers drop a line and sit there. Sometimes they sit for hours, waiting for that hungry fish to grab their delicious bait and get hooked.

We used to get hooked by the bait of compulsive gambling. But, we found that getting caught by its hook was leading us to our death. Unlike those fish, we were able to escape. And each day we work our program is another day that hook can't catch us.

~

I am grateful to be free from the hook of compulsive gambling. I am free.

April 16

The loss which is unknown is no loss at all.

PUBILIUS SYRUS

Each day people lose thousands of things—pencils, keys, letters, and, of course, thoughts. We scour every nook and cranny opening drawers, pulling out furniture, and putting our bodies in all sorts of unusual contortions to search. If we're lucky, we find that missing item or thought.

We are lucky. Maybe that key or pen is still missing after all our looking. It doesn't matter. We found a treasure worth much more.

Our lives. They were lost to our compulsive gambling. Through working our recovery program, we have found our life. And we work each day to keep it found.

~

I was lost, but now I'm found.
I am happy to have this glorious treasure—my life.

April 17

It may be ahead of its time, but it's still in touch with your needs
ADVERTISEMENT FOR AUTOMOBILE

Sue tells the group of her entry into gambling. "My husband died unexpectedly, I was working many hours the bank, I hadn't had a vacation in ages and I was ill. Nothing like this would have happened if I hadn't been ill at the time. They should have seen through my behavior. I had never stolen anything before."

Excuses. Plain and simple excuses. If Sue's husband hadn't died, if she'd worked less and vacationed more. If she felt better, would she have still gambled? Maybe, maybe not. If it hadn't been these triggers, there would have been others. Was she ill because she gambled or did she gamble because she was ill?

The fact is, we gambled. And we lost. But it isn't that way any more. Each day that we work our program, we find that the excuses don't matter. What does matter is that we have identified the underlying causes of our compulsive gambling addiction and are working through our issues.

~

I am happy to be free from the destruction gambling brings. I will focus my energy today on growing in my recovery. I am getting in touch with my feelings and needs.

April 18

I can't do it for them. I have to do it for me.

JASON

Please don't gamble anymore," Jason's wife Betty pleaded, "I can't take it anymore." The truth is Betty couldn't take it anymore. Jason's gambling has gotten totally out of control. It was wrecking their marriage.

Although Jason certainly has Betty to consider, his decision to enter into a recovery program was one he had to come to terms with on his own. Reluctantly, Jason determined that he needed help. Once in his program, however, Jason began to see the results of a life free from gambling. His work paid off in the relief he experienced in his recovery program.

~

I respect the needs of my family.
However, I know my recovery has to come from me.

April 19

The road to success is paved with detours.
Follow a plan and check your course.
SAYING ON A PLAQUE

In recovery, we actively work on the 12 steps in our program. We know the steps, followed in order and worked one at a time, lead us forward in our release from compulsive gambling. Lucky for us this is a program where we start to heal from the moment we take that first step. We know this is not a program where we complete 12 steps and with a snap of the fingers, we are cured.

As we work our program, there will be times when we aren't progressing as quickly as we think we should. At times like this, we must remember that we didn't get sick overnight. And, we aren't going to get better in one day. Rather, we get better every day we work our program.

The road to recovery is paved with challenges.
It is also lined with victory in our goal of
freedom from compulsive gambling.

April 20

I detest that man, who hides one thing in the depths of his heart, and speaks forth another.

HOMER

C.J. never lets anyone see her without her make up on and every hair in place. Not even to work in the yard or pick up the mail. After all, what would others think if she wasn't at her best?

Is she covering up the "real" her? Is she striving for perfection?

That the way it was for us when we gambled. We were forever covering up. How wonderful it is for us to be free from the chains of lies and striving for perfection. How great it feels to have taken off all the camouflage and bared our souls.

~

I do try to look my best and know that's ok
I do it to complement how I feel about myself
on the inside. I will not use it to cover up
the beautiful person I am.

April 21

The innocent is the person who explains nothing.

ALBERT CAMUS

Six year old Zach and his aunt were carving up the turkey. "Here," said Auntie, "you can take the wishbone home."

With a look of absolute disgust and an impatient wave of his hand, Zach brushed off this silly thought. "Throw it away," he said, "I don't want any old chicken bones."

Ah, the innocence of a child. And how wonderful to see things through their beautiful eyes. Let's remember to stop and take a look.

~

Today I will remember to stop and get in touch
with my inner child. I will take a fresh look
at things through new eyes.

April 22

He who yields a prudent obedience, exercises a partial control.

PUBLILIUS SYRUS

Have you ever traveled by plane and spent the entire day waiting? You've done your part—booked reservations in advance, arrived at the airport an hour before departure and checked in at the gate well ahead of boarding time. All your pieces are in place.

But the outcome isn't what you wanted. You are tired of waiting. And disappointed.

Let go and let God. We can't control outcomes. We can only do our part and let our Higher Power guide us. Yes, our pieces were in place. And we should feel good about doing our part.

~

I know that when I do my best,
I can be proud of my actions.
The outcome is not up to me.

April 23

If individuality has no play, society does not advance . . . .
THOMAS HENRY HUXLEY

After rolling out the dough, the baker uses a cookie cutter to make sure that each cookie comes out exactly like the next. They all have the same shape and will be baked to the same golden brown color.

People aren't like those cookies. We each have our own likes and dislikes. We are getting in touch with our feelings for the first time in our lives. No longer are we living by someone else's rules, trying to be exactly like them.

~

I am no longer in the mold others have placed me in.
I am free to be me, to discover how wonderful I am.

April 24

Recovery is support—from those who care about your recovery; from those who care about you.

SHELLEY

The tightrope walker balances carefully on the wire. Each step is measured. Mind and body are working together in determined concentration. One misstep could send him plummeting. Below him is a safety net to catch his fall, should he become unbalanced and need some help.

We have our own safety net in our recovery. Around us are many who support us in our efforts to remain free from the horrors of gambling.

I am thankful for the support I receive.
I will remember help is just a phone call away
should I begin to feel unbalanced.

April 25

I used to think I needed expensive things to make me comfortable.
Trouble was, I never was comfortable.

JOAN D.

Jo is forty years old. An she has a favorite blanket. You see, Jo's great grandmother used to make quilts. Soft, comforting, homemade quilts.

When Jo is feeling stressed or sad and needs some time out, she wraps herself in that quilt. She feels a soothing peace. She feels safe. She feels the love of her great grandmother.

There's nothing wrong with a 40 year old having a favorite blanket. There's nothing wrong with anyone, any age, wrapping themselves in the peace and serenity of recovery.

~

Today I will remind myself that I am
safe in the serenity of my program.
I am comforted by my recovery process.

April 26

Here's a quarter (call someone who cares).

TRAVIS TRITT SONG

Sometimes it seems like no one cares. We're out of sorts, but we don't know exactly what is wrong. We want some attention, but no one seems to notice.

Why not? We think we're sending others signals. How can they not know how we feel?

They don't know because we haven't told them. We think we're sending out beacons of feelings that alert others to our needs. We have to put those feelings into words. They're our feelings, not others.

~

I know others can't read my mind.
I take responsibility for my feelings
and letting others know my needs.

April 27

Habit, my friend, is practice long pursued,
that at last becomes the man himself.

EVENUS

Everything we hear today is recycle, recycle, recycle. No longer do we throw out those newspapers, cans and plastics.

We need to practice recycling in our program, too. Over and over again we use our twelve steps to help us stay on the path to health and serenity. Like product recycling, our program feels awkward at first, but the longer we walk our talk, the more comfortable and natural our life in recovery feels.

~

I know it is important to use the steps
of my program over and over. In doing so,
I am finding the peace and happiness I deserve.

April 28

Made a decision to turn our will and our lives over to the care of this power of our own understanding.

STEP 3

We know help is available to us. But knowing it and using that help are two different things.

Our determination to remain free from gambling enables us to make the choice to trust in our Higher Power. And to show our faith in our Higher Power's ability to help us, we put our life in his or her hands.

Our decision was the right one. Every day we grow more solid in our commitment to remain free from gambling.

~

I am positive my decision to work with
my Higher Power was the correct one.
I will let my Higher Power guide me in my recovery.

April 29

I tried not to listen. I thought I knew everything.

JASON

Before an airplane takes off, passengers are routinely treated to a Federal Aviation Administration safety talk. Flight attendants show passengers where exits are and explain all safety precautions.

For the person who travels a lot, it's easy to tune this part of the trip out. They think "Yeah, we've heard it all before. I don't need to listen."

Sometimes in recovery, we think we have heard it all before, too. We can get arrogant about listening to our recovery program messages.

Maybe we have heard it all before. But, we need to pay attention and heed the warning signs. Because if we get too grandiose about our recovery, we can easily slip back into the unhealthy patterns of our compulsive gambling.

~

I will pay attention to my recovery. I will work my program and be aware of the warning signs.

April 30

By trading in our impatience for peace of mind
we have sold out not to the devil.

ALAN HARRINGTON

"I want it now," screams the child, "I don't want to wait until later." Impatiently, the child continues to try to convince his parents to give in.

We, too, can get impatient. We want to be well NOW. We don't want to spend one more day in recovery. We want our peace and serenity. And we want it this minute.

We have to remember at times like this that we didn't get to be compulsive gamblers yesterday. It was built up over time—from childhood. There is no instant cure for recovery from compulsive gambling. The recovery process is ongoing—one day at a time.

My recovery depends on my commitment in
my program. Each day of my life—one day at a time.

May 1

A man's behavior is the index of the man,
and his discourse is the index of his understanding.
ALI IBN-ABI-TALIB

Listeners of talk radio shows know that there is a seven second delay between the time a caller says something and when it is heard over the radio. This is done so that inappropriate remarks can be blocked before they are passed over the air waves, possibly offending some listeners.

Wouldn't it be nice if there were a delay between the time we exhibit inappropriate behavior and when it is seen by others. Perhaps we acted in a grandiose manner, embarrassing ourselves and those around us. With the delay feature, we could "block out" our mistakes.

We don't have that luxury, though. The behavior we display is exactly what gets seen by everyone.

~

I will remember to think before acting.
I will make sure my behavior
reflects the actions I want it to.

May 2

A man cannot be comfortable without his own approval.

MARK TWAIN

For those living in northern climates, winter can bring sub-zero temperatures on a daily basis. One of the most peaceful things on a chilly night is to crawl into bed surrounding your body with a cozy quilt. It seems as if your body is wrapped in warmth and caring.

Just as quilts on a cold night can be soothing, so is our recovery program. It, too, surrounds us—with peace, calm and serenity. Recovery wraps us in the tender comfort of a life without the ruin of compulsive gambling. Recovery is a place where we are safe.

I am happy to be wrapped in the comfort
of my recovery program. I know I must
do my own work, but it is great to know
I am surrounded by the support of recovery.

May 3

I felt if I could get someone else to make the decisions,
I wouldn't be accountable. I could blame them.

SYLVIA

What's preventing you from making a decision today? Is it fear of failure? Fear of the unknown? Fear that you can't control the outcome? Fear of taking the risk?

In times like this, it's important to remember that we don't have any control over outcomes. None. Zero. Zip.

We do have control over our part in the process of making that decision. If we feel we have done our best, then whatever the outcome, we can be pleased with the part we played in it.

~

I will remember that I don't have to be afraid
to make decisions. I will do my best.
That's all I will ever ask of me.

May 4

Knowledge may give weight, but accomplishments give luster,
and many more people see than weigh.

LORD CHESTERFIELD

June is the month of graduations. Graduations from high school or from college. Sometimes there are even graduations from kindergarten and elementary school grades. Whatever the graduation event, it marks an important time in a person's life.

Working our recovery program can be considered a graduation, too. By applying ourselves to change the destructive behaviors we lived daily while actively gambling, we can remove ourselves from a life of lies, cheating and devastation. We graduate into a life of honesty. With ourselves and others.

~

I am thankful for my graduation
from compulsive gambling and into recovery.

May 5

A journey of a thousand miles must begin with a single step.
CHINESE PROVERB

Sometimes a baby's first steps are honored by their parents casting their first pair of walking shoes in bronze. This represents a milestone in the baby's life.

Many of us have less ornamental representations of some of the milestones of our youth. But, they are symbolic all the same. Those of us who were mistreated, heard continually demeaning words, got angry looks or even have marks of physical abuse are all too aware of the landmarks of our turbulent growing years.

But, now we are taking a different kind of baby steps. Each step we take in recovery is a positive step in our development of freedom from the addiction of compulsive gambling. Each day we work our program is a milestone in our life of serenity.

~

I will remember that each bit of progress I make—
each step I take—is a milestone in my recovery.

May 6

"It is in your act that you exist, not in your body.
Your act is yourself, and there is no other you."
SAINT-EXUPERY

Actors and actresses play roles that are make believe. In order to successfully pull off the role they are hired for, they need to pretend to be something they aren't. At times it may even seem awkward for them, but with hours and days of rehearsals, they can perform as expected by the director.

When we enter our recovery program and even at times further into our program, we may feel like we are "acting out" the new, healthy behaviors. That's because they are still unfamiliar to us and, perhaps, a bit uncomfortable.

But, as we practice them over and over, they will become more comfortable to us. After a while, they will even come naturally. Until that time, we just need to remember to "bring the body and the mind will follow."

I know that although some of my new behaviors
are uncomfortable, they will become natural
to me as I grow in recovery.

May 7

I do love booze and women.

JON

Sometimes we feel we are working our program if we are abstaining from gambling. We may not have been in a casino in months. We place no bets anymore. We're cured.

But, we may be substituting other destructive behaviors for our gambling abstinence. Are we drinking more? Do we have an insatiable sexual appetite? Do we recant endlessly religious sayings? Are we exercising beyond what is healthy? Have we transferred the loss of gambling to another addiction?

As recovering individuals, we need to remind ourselves that gambling may not be our only addiction. We may have one or more others that are surfacing more strongly. Maybe drinking has taken a place in our lives as the number one addiction at this point.

Let's remember that recovery means abstinence. From all behaviors that throw our lives in that cruel cycle of unmanageability. Let's remember to release ourselves from this destruction.

Today, I will look at my life and ask myself
if there are other addictions that need addressing.

May 8

I will work towards eliminating all self-destructive behavior from my life.

HATILETT FINGERMAN

We can't go through a treatment program once and be cured from our compulsive gambling addiction. There is no cure for compulsive gambling.

Treatment may be a first step. It can't stop there. For if it does, we may slip. We become a standing target for the things that led us to compulsive gambling.

We don't want to become a bulls eye for the gambling arrow. So we have to keep moving. Not rushing, moving. A step at a time. Some days it will be a baby step. Other days, we'll take a big step. It doesn't matter.

What does matter is that we keep moving. For when we do, we move farther forward in our recovery program. And the gambling arrow will miss us every time.

~

I will take one step further in my recovery today. Even if it is a baby step. Even if I feel like I am crawling instead of stepping, I will remember that I am moving in a positive direction.

May 9

Good health is more than just exercise and diet.
It's really a point of view and a mental attitude.
You can have the strongest body,
but it's not good unless the person inside of you
has strength and optimism.

ANGELA LANSBURY

We exercise like crazy. We cut out the fats and eat good food. Are we healthy?

It may appear so on the outside. Our bodies may be trim and our hair may be shiny. Maybe we can do 150 sit-ups. But, what about our insides? Are we taking care of those, too?

Real health and wellness means focusing on our total health. Making sure that we are in tune with our feelings. Dealing with the many issues that have haunted us and led to our destructive compulsive gambling behavior. Working through the pain and ensuring our progress in recovery one step at a time.

~

I will make sure I take care of myself inside and out.
My health depends on it.

May 10

It's harder to hit a moving target.
I think people should keep moving, moving, moving.
I just think it's time we stopped operating full time out of fear
and boundaries and old images, and stepped out and showed ourselves.

ALI MACGRAW

Gambling controlled us. It robbed us of our dignity. We hated what it had done to our lives. It destroyed our relationships and drove us to the brink of bankruptcy and suicide. Our lives were unmanageable. We operated in total fear. Of everything and everyone.

In recovery we are taking a look at ourselves, our emotions and our feelings. We are not gambling. We are breaking down those old boundaries of shame and fear. Each day we think less and less about gambling and more and more about recovery.

Each day the boundaries of self destruction
are breaking down. In their place, I am putting up
healthy boundaries, for my highest good.

May 11

Bit by bit, I am ridding my life of undesirable behaviors.

DICK

There is something called the onion theory. We all know an onion has many layers. As we continue to peel away those layers, the smell gets harsher.

In recovery, we are like an onion. We continue to peel away the layers of our life of devastation. Layer by layer we begin to deal with our issues one by one. We work through the lies, the cheating, the grandiosity. We keep peeling until we have faced our problems. And as we peel away the layers, we begin to rebuild our lives.

~

I am peeling away the layers of my life
of destruction and building my life of peace.

May 12

For what in your life do you feel most grateful?

GREGORY STOCK, PH.D.

For some time, we had a love-hate relationship with gambling. We loved the excitement, the thrill of the big win. But there was a dark side to gambling. We hated to lose. We hated to lie. We hated to cover up. Bills piled up. We borrowed money. But, it was never enough. We hated this vicious cycle we were in.

How wonderful that we have a true love relationship with recovery. For it has given us the freedom from hate and that horrible life we tried to unsuccessfully live. We are now supported by a program that offers us a relationship with all that is good and healthy. We have found new friends to help us stay positive and involved in our new-found lives.

~

Today, I will remind myself that I am
in a loving, supportive relationship with recovery.
I am thankful for my new friends and my new life.

May 13

Made a searching and fearless moral and
financial inventory of ourselves.

STEP 4

We have to deal with our past. All true hope for our future lies in this step. Because it's time to clean house. To look at those people in our lives that we have caused harm.

We have to face the guilt we are experiencing. Because facing this guilt will allow us to release it. And releasing it will allow us to take another step, give us another victory in our recovery.

Whether or not I have reached my step 4,
I recognize it's completion will signal a
success in my personal recovery program.

May 14

(About women) They're wonderful—they're amazing creatures. You can never learn enough . . . . They have so many levels.

ROBIN WILLIAMS

Fashion models tell stories of starving themselves to maintain their "image." To be marketable to others. It all ends in self-destruction.

How many times have we, too, compromised our values and morals for "image?" How many times have we covered up who we are, how we feel?

Thank goodness it doesn't have to be like that anymore. We can stop covering up who we are. Our image means living our morals and our values. It means being who we are. It means we are good enough.

I will look myself in the mirror and say,
"I am a wonderful person. I am good enough.
I love myself."

May 15

The greatest of all mistakes is to do nothing because you can only do a little. Do what you can.

SYDNEY SMITH

In some states, winter means an onslaught of snow and ice. It continues to build up from November through March. Sometimes light, fluffy flakes fall. Sometimes the snow comes in blizzards, adding inches in a short time period.

Then Spring comes. Gradually the days get warmer and warmer. The sun stays in the sky longer and longer. Does the snow vanish in one day? One week? No, it melts away a little at a time.

Now, just as we have taken years in our life to build up our self-destructive behavior, we will need to focus our recovery process from compulsive gambling for the rest of our lives. Overwhelming? It doesn't have to be. We can do a little—every day—to grow in our personal recovery process.

~

I will remember that my recovery means taking little steps. Each day builds on the strength I am gaining in my program.

May 16

How would you like a job where, if you make a mistake,
a big red light goes on and 18,000 people boo?
JACQUES PLANTE

In life, we make many mistakes. In recovery, we make mistakes. It isn't a perfect world. Even in doing our personal best, we will, at times, make poor decisions, take inappropriate actions, say hurtful things.

This doesn't give us open license to brush off the mistakes we make. We can't excuse our mistakes. But, we can learn from them. We can use these blips in our recovery process to build on and help us grow stronger.

~

Each time I make a mistake, I will not make excuses.
I will not berate myself. I will use the situation
to learn from—and to grow.

May 17

It takes a whole village to raise a child.

AFRICAN PROVERB

We're working our program. Sure, some days, making more progress than other days. The important thing is we are making progress every day we remain clean.

We don't have to do it alone. Sure, we have our individual work to do, but we are surrounded by a wonderful support system. There are many others working their recovery programs, too. In addition, many professionals in compulsive gambling treatment are available.

I know I am working my individual program.
I am surrounded by a supportive recovery system.

May 18

Treat others the way they want to be treated.

SAM

All our lives we've heard the golden rule "do unto others as you would have them do unto you." How can we possibly know that what we want is also what another person would like. Maybe they don't want to be treated the way we want to be treated.

Just as we are determining our boundaries, we need to be aware of others' boundaries. We must be respectful of what others' needs are. We may not be able to live with their boundaries, but we recognize their right to establish their life choices.

Its important to recognize that others' boundaries may not be the same as mine. I will decide what is right for me and respect their right to choose, too.

May 19

When did you last sing to yourself? To someone else?

GREGORY STOCK, PH.D.

We've said good bye to gambling. It used to rip our lives apart. We spent a lot of time trying to fit our lives into the gambling way of life—lies, fear, shame.

Now, its going to be our way. Without the lies. Without the shame. We have taken back our lives. We have faced our shame. And with it, we've gained a new friend—ourselves. We've gained someone we can really trust—ourselves. We can sing the praises of our own hard work in our recovery process.

Today, I will remember the joy I have found in recovery. I am glad to have "me" back.

May 20

By dignity, I mean the high place attained
only when the heart and mind are lifted,
equally at once, by the creative union
of perception and grace.
JAMES THURBER

All people, no matter what, deserve to be treated with dignity. We may have made poor choices while we were gambling, but our most important choice—the decision to seek help—shows we are able to distinguish right from wrong.

No, we can't brush off our mistakes. Or pretend they didn't matter. Of course, we know they did. We can't take that back. But, despite our shortcomings, we are worthy of dignity.

Although people make mistakes,
they deserve to be treated with dignity.
I deserve to be treated with dignity.

May 21

It takes a happy person to create a happy book.

LAVYRLE SPENCER

Happiness can mean various things to people. A bright sun coming up in the morning can bring a smile to our face. Getting a well-deserved raise will certainly make us happy.

Happiness in recovery has one meaning. To all of us, it is the pleasure we experience day after day in living a life of peace and serenity. Knowing that each step we take in our recovery program brings us deeper joy. That is true happiness.

~

I am happy to be progressing in my recovery program.
I am happy to have found serenity.

May 22

Often we are firm from weakness . . . .

LA ROUCHE

The first months in recovery are like riding a roller coaster. Sometimes it seems like for every step we take forward, we are taking two backwards.

Thank goodness our personal recovery program is our seatbelt. By working our program every day, we stay firmly fastened in the seat of progress.

~

My first days in recovery may seem shaky,
but working my program
will keep me steady in recovery.

May 23

Refrain tonight, and that shall lend a kind of easiness
to the next abstinence; the next more easy;
for use almost can change the stamp of nature.
SHAKESPEARE

The media perpetuates gambling. It is in magazines, on television and radio. We see scratch off cards at the fast food places. Gambling is everywhere in our lives.

How do we abstain from gambling when is it continually thrown in our face? By working our program, that's how. Whenever we feel ourselves wavering, we call our support system. Every step we take forward in our program helps us to grow stronger in our will to remain free from gambling.

After a while, we will feel comfortable tuning out those television and radio spots, paging past the ads in magazines and returning those scratch off cards at the fast food place with a "No thanks, but have a nice day."

~

I can't control the media coverage on gambling,
but I can control my reaction. As I grown in recovery,
I am becoming stronger in my resistance to gambling.

May 24

Compassion for the friend should conceal itself under a hard shell.

NIETZSCHE

Jan sat in her boss' office crying. Between heartbreaking sobs, she told her boss the details of her crisis. "Yesterday was our five-year-old's birthday. All the pieces were in place—food prepared, family coming, presents bought."

"But, Jim, my husband didn't show up, as he promised he would. The night before, he left for a quick trip to the casino. Hours later, he still hadn't returned. He ended up missing our daughter's party. I was so hurt, and humiliated, in front of our families."

Jan's boss, a recovering compulsive gambler, fought off the urge to preach on the disaster of gambling. After all, her boss knew promise for promise, how a gambler acts.

The boss didn't preach. She also knew firsthand how painful living with a gambler is.

~

I remember the pain compulsive gambling brings.
I will be compassionate to others in pain,
while acknowledging their need to do their own work.

May 25

Once you become aware, you can never become unaware.

STEVE J.

We may be tempted at times to just give up. We're working our program, but it doesn't seem to be going as fast as we want it to. Perhaps we've had thoughts of calling it quits and returning to gambling.

Don't. We know recovery works. We've had successes in our program. Some have been big. More often, they are small. We must remember, though, we have success every day we refrain from gambling and work our program.

We are aware that recovery works. We know recovery gives us the peace and serenity we want. We are also aware that compulsive gambling doesn't work.

~

Once we became aware recovery works,
we can now never become unaware
of the serenity it provides.

May 26

We cannot direct the wind, but we can adjust the sails.

SAYING ON A PLAQUE

Outcomes are beyond our control. We do, however, have responsibility for our actions. In recovery, this means working our program every day. Making sure we're taking the necessary actions to ensure we remain clean.

Our healthy actions in recovery include not only abstaining from active gambling, but also changing the behaviors that led us to gambling. In doing so, we can be assured we will continue our growth in recovery.

~

Although I have no control over outcomes,
I know that by working my program
I will continue to grow in recovery.

May 27

As soon as the people fix one Shame of the World, another turns up.

EDGAR WATSON HOWE

Compulsive gambling is not about being a bad person. It is about being a good person who is shame-based. And the way we dealt with that shame was gambling.

Gambling started out creating the highs for us. A sense of winning, being in control. But it didn't continue and we created more shame for ourselves by lying, stealing, cheating.

Recovery helps us identify our source of shame and work on ridding ourselves of the untruths we were told about ourselves. Recovery helps us get off the roller coaster of highs and lows. It lets us face that shame based system head on.

~

I am eliminating the shame in my life.
I am a worthy human being.

May 28

Courage is the thing. All goes if courage goes.

J. M. BARRIE

Recovery is not a piece of cake. It does not just fall into our lives and suddenly cure us, making us forever happy. It takes work; at times a lot of work.

But, it goes beyond working our program. It requires courage. Courage to face our issues. Courage to stay with our personal recovery program when it seems to be a major struggle. Courage to stand up to those around us who are uncomfortable with our victory over compulsive gambling. Courage just to keep moving ahead.

So we must stop from time to time and just think about the courage we have shown. We have to acknowledge the courage we have to draw upon at times to ensure we continue to live a life free from addiction.

~

I have the courage to work my program.
I have the courage to move forward in my personal recovery.

May 29

There is no useful rule without an exception.

THOMAS FULLER, M.D.

Roller skates have four wheels—two each in the front and back, with a bumper knob in the front. In order to take off, a skater needs to use the front to launch himself. Likewise, in order to stop, the skater needs to use that front bumper knob to assist him.

In-line skates changed all the rules. Typically four or five wheels are arranged single file on the skates. The stop bumper is located on the back of the boot. To take off the skater needs to push off from the side and to stop, he must drag his foot on the back bumper knob.

The roles in life have changed for us, too, in recovery. Before beginning our personal recovery journey, the rules were physical and emotional withdrawal, excuses, shame and anger. Now, in recovery, there are new rules for healthy living: abstinence from gambling, truth, honesty, defining our values, and becoming self-responsible.

~

Types of skating are a matter of personal preference.
Neither one is better than the other. However,
when it comes to gambling or recovery,
I know the clear choice for me is recovery.

May 30

I didn't know what boundaries were.
I didn't know I had a right to my own.
SHELIA J.

In the game of moonlight bowling, lights over the lanes are turned off. Bowlers are then expected to knock the lighted pins down without any lane boundaries to judge their bowling by.

Moonlight bowling is just a game. It shows that sometimes it is fun to play without boundaries, in the appropriate place. Our personal recovery journey, though, helps us establish boundaries. Throughout our lives, we've been unable to set boundaries for ourselves. It's important to our progress in recovery to know our boundaries and live our lives according to them. If we do, we'll get a strike in life every time.

~

Healthy boundaries are important to my growth.
I will identify them for myself.

May 31

If a man is devout, we accuse him of hypocrisy;
if he is not, of impiety; if he is humble,
we look on his humility as a weakness . . . .
LOUIS BOURDALOUE

Being humble doesn't come easy to gamblers. After living a life of grandiosity, humble isn't something we easily know how to be. It's important for use to learn how to be humble, though. Living in the pretentious world of grandiosity kept us in the deadly grasp of fantasy. Always trying to let others think we're bigger than we are. Always trying to convince ourselves it was really true.

Serenity isn't grand. Serenity is tranquility. It's calming and it brings peace of mind.

~

Being humble allows me to be truthful.
It relieves us from the trap of grandiosity.

June 1

Trust that man in nothing who has not a conscience in everything.

LAURENCE STERNE

Promises, promises. During our gambling days we were great at making promises. Problem was, we weren't good at keeping promises.

We know promises are easy to make. What counts is our ability to follow through. It's important that we do just that. Because as we begin to keep the promises we make, however small, we can be counted on. As we build our credibility, others will begin to renew their trust in us.

I know I am trustworthy.
As I keep my promises to others,
they will know I am trustworthy, too.

June 2

Virtue herself is her own fairest reward.

SFLIUS ITALICUS

Immediate gratification through taking risks used to be our way of life. In an attempt to make up for our losses, we gambled again, even though we had lost shortly before. Or, we may have abruptly changed or interrupted our plans to pursue our gambling plans.

Recovery taught us that rewards are ours. But, they aren't always instant. True, lasting gratification comes from steadily working our program. And continually receiving the rewards of serenity.

~

Satisfaction with my life comes from
the progress I make in recovery.

June 3

Compromise, such an adjustment of conflicting interests as gives each adversary the satisfaction of thinking he has got what he ought not to have, and is deprived of nothing except what was justly his due.

AMBROSE PIERCE

Before beginning our recovery program, we were spiritually bankrupt. Along the road to our bankruptcy, we made many compromises. We compromised our honesty and the ability to be honest with ourselves. We compromised trust and our being perceived as trustworthy. We compromised the respect of others and our own self-respect. We compromised emotional support. We compromised fairness and equity.

But, after a time, we could no longer rationalize our gambling behavior and blame others. We began to face ourselves and gradually we made deposits into our spirituality account.

~

In recovery, I know as long as I work my program, my spirituality account will never be empty again.

June 4

The best preparation for good work tomorrow is to do good work today.

ELBERT HUBBARD

In this technologically advanced society, there is computer software for every need imaginable. Want to do your taxes? Get some software for under $100. It does your taxes just like an accountant.

Need to write a letter? There's a selection of over 30 word processing software systems. Want to design an invitation? The shelves display many fancy, easy to use graphics packages.

But, the program we can't buy in a computer store is our recovery program. It can't be bought in any store. Because we can't load recovery software into a computer, press a few keys and—presto!—we are cured.

We have to work our own program. We load it into our internal system step by step, day by day. There are no quick cures.

~

Computers can help us in a lot of ways.
But, they can't work my recovery program for me.
I must do that for myself.

June 5

Usually when people are sad, they don't do anything.
They just cry over their condition.

MALCOLM X

At times, we all feel "blue." We may be a bit sad or our spirits may be low, but in a very short period of time, we are back to our old selves.

At other times, we may also experience a period of time where we just can't seem to shake our blues. We are lethargic, have trouble sleeping, can't concentrate and maybe even think about suicide or death. Perhaps this feeling has been going on for a month or more.

This is depression. It, too, has many forms—severe, moderate and mild. If it lasts longer than a month, we need to seek help from a professional. Getting help doesn't mean we're crazy. In fact, it means we are very much sane, because we recognize we need help—and get it.

~

I am aware of the symptoms of depression.
I will look at my life for any signs and seek help.

June 6

You will never find time for anything.
If you want time you must make it.
CHARLES BUXTON

Our serenity is essential to a healthy life. Each minute we spend living our program is a minute more that we find that peace we've been searching for forever. A life without constant surprises. A life without chaos. A life without continual up and down emotions.

What does this life of joy cost us? Devotion to working our program on a daily basis. When we keep our focus on our goal of tranquility in our life, the cost seems small. For we are supported each step of the way in our program. We know exactly what our program promises us if only we will take the action. It is a promise we know we can count on, unlike many other promises that have been made to us in our life. When we trust recovery, we trust in our Higher Power to guide us. We also trust in ourself to see the importance of the work we do and the responsibility we have to work our program. We know we've made the right decision.

~

I trust the work I do leads me forward
in my life of recovery. I trust myself
to take my responsibility seriously
for the sake of my sanity.

June 7

Life isn't a matter of milestones, but of moments.
ROSE KENNEDY

We worry a lot about the future. When we make enough money, we'll have all our bills paid off. When we get to the weekend, we won't have to deal with this job. When we get to tomorrow, we'll be done with this work project.

What happens when we live in the future is we forget about the here and now. What's happening with us today? Are we working our program so that we ensure our freedom from compulsive gambling? Are we meeting with our sponsor this hour to work through our struggles and frustrations? Do we stop for this one minute to congratulate ourselves for having the courage and commitment to give our life over to our Higher Power, knowing that the serenity that comes from recovery is worth far more than the fleeting high we felt from a few moments of gambling?

Each moment of each day is ours to use. It is up to us to use it wisely. To use it to further our progress in our recovery program.

~

I will use each moment I have today
to work my program. I know my moments
will become my future by themselves.

June 8

Unmerited abuse wounds . . .

THOMAS JEFFERSON

Compulsive gambling is about substance abuse. The substance is money. And, of course, we abused money by gambling it away.

We may at times feel that others don't recognize compulsive gambling as an addiction. They can't smell it on our breath. Our eyes aren't glazed over. We can speak without slurring.

We need to stay away from getting into a confrontation about compulsive gambling. We know it's a legitimate addiction. We know we work every day to keep ourselves clean.

At times when I am frustrated over others' lack of knowledge about compulsive gambling, I will find the encouragement I need in my support system.

June 9

The measure of a man's real character is
what he would do if he knew he would never be found out.
T. B. MACAULAY

We have many opportunities each and every day to prove we have integrity. When we call in sick to work are we really too ill to work? Or, do we just use that as an excuse so we don't have to go in? When that sales associate gives us back too much change for our purchase, do we figure it is her tough luck and keep it? Or do we return it? When our child asks us to play with them, do we snap at them and say we are too busy? Or do we understand that our child needs a few minutes of our attention?

Integrity is within us. No one can force us to have it. No one can force us to use it. It is a decision we make for ourselves. Integrity is living our life honestly. It is following through on our commitments. It is telling the truth. It is being reliable.

When we have integrity, others know it. They know they can trust us in any situation. That doesn't mean they will always agree with us. But, they will understand that we live our life honorably. They can count on it. That's integrity.

~

I live my life with integrity. I will consider the actions
I take today to ensure integrity my life.

June 10

Beauty's where you find it.
MADONNA

"Man, it's cold out today. The wind is blowing and I am just freezing," complains Joe to his co-workers. "When will we get some decent weather? I'm tired of this stuff."

In another conversation, Susan is talking excitedly to her friends. "Isn't this sun beautiful? Look at how it reflects off the pond. The cool, crisp water looks like a mirror. This is unbelievable!"

It is the same weather. But, each has a different attitude. Our attitude on life is our key to creating the life we want. If we constantly think doom and gloom that is exactly the kind of life we are creating for ourselves. On the other hand, if we can look at our life, struggles and all, and see that glimmer of hope and happiness shining through, we will find ourselves enjoying life more. Today is ours. How will we live it? The choice is also ours.

~

I choose to live today positively.
I choose happiness.

June 11

It is o.k. to work my program. It is not o.k. to work someone else's.

JEANNETTE

After being involved in our recovery program for a time, it is easy for us to think we are the resident experts in the field of compulsive gambling and recovery.

Helping others is important. But, just as important is allowing others to actually work there own recovery program. We must be careful to ensure what we consider helping does not actually interfere with another's recovery progress.

We are learning a lot of the answers for ourselves. But, we don't have the answers for others. Recovery will guide them in their process to find their own answers. As recovering gamblers ourselves, we can support their process, knowing that support means letting them do the work.

~

I will look to ensure that my enthusiasm
over my success in recovery does not interfere
with another's ability to work their own program.

June 12

The only place you'll find success before work is in the dictionary.

MAY B. SMITH

To be successful, all you have to do is have this beautiful hair, which you can get by using our hair products. To be successful, stop in and buy this expensive automobile. Then, everyone will know right away what a success you are. To be successful, wear this designer suit. It just screams success.

If success were this easy, everyone in the world would be successful. We wouldn't have to worry about money or relationships or commitments. Life would be a cinch.

We know, however, success is rarely immediate. When we think about the successful people in our life, we know they have worked hard for that success. They were willing to do whatever was necessary in order to ensure their success. We also understand that success is more than material goods. It is a way of life.

As we work our program, we know that the steps we are taking, however big or small, are ensuring our success in recovery. We understand that all the hard work we're doing leads us forward in recovery.

~

I am committed to doing my work
so that I continue to have the serenity
I find in recovery.

June 13

The one thing that doesn't abide
by majority rule is a person's conscience."

HARPER LEE

Often we are coaxed to try something we don't want to. Maybe it is that new recipe for broccoli casserole. It could be that movie that has too much violence in it for us. Or, it might be running five miles when we're just beginning our physical fitness program.

Sometimes, it is much more serious, like joining our friends at the casino. We know we can't go because we are purposely placing ourselves in danger. That little voice in our head tells us not to go. Our friends tell us to go. What do we do?

We make the decision that is best for us, that's what we do. If we go, we know we put our recovery in jeopardy. We will undermine all the work we've done to remain free from the clutches of gambling. Why would we want to do that?

We must listen to our conscience. We know what is best for ourselves in this situation. Our friends do not. We've chosen the road to recovery. We must continue to walk that path to ensure the peace we have found.

~

I will listen to my conscience.
I know it will keep in on the road to recovery.

June 14

Learn by practice.

MARTHA GRAHAM

The first pages of this book didn't come easy. We knew what we wanted to say, but how would we get them down on paper? We wrote a few pages. Then, we went back and rewrote the pages. Sometimes, we even went back and rewrote the pages another time.

It is the same way for people entering their recovery program. Recovery is so unfamiliar to us. We know gambling. As impossible as a life of gambling was to live, we have to admit we knew how to live it. We were exceptional liars. It doesn't mean we were happy with ourselves, but we certainly knew how to do it.

In recovery, we learn to stick with it. It may be strange to us at first. We want to work through the pain we feel, but it is so difficult.

We have to believe it will get easier. Each time we tell the truth, it gets easier to tell the truth the next time. The truth feels good, even when it is difficult. Each time we work through our pain, we understand the hurt we've lived for so long. It gets easier to face that pain. We only need to keep practicing until it is no longer practice. It is the way we live.

~

Today, I will practice the steps in my recovery program. I know they are important to my serenity.

June 15

The truth is just as meaningful as the lie.

A CLICHÉ

Truth is a new way of life for us. We've told so many lies in the past, we didn't even know how to tell the truth. It sometimes seems amazing it could have been like that, but we know it is true.

The lies we told were important. Because each time we told a lie, we were actually saying to others that we could not be trusted. Our words reinforced that we did not have any integrity.

The truths we speak today are just as important. For with each truth we tell, we are letting others know that we understand our past behavior and we are committed to changing that behavior. We are succeeding in changing each time we tell the truth and we stick to that truth. Others then begin to see us as an honest person, one they can count on.

~

Today I will speak only the truth.
I am the truth.

June 16

Suppose a great person takes the risk and fails. Then the person must try again. You cannot fail forever. If you try ten times, you have a better chance of making it on the eleventh try than if you didn't try at all.

ARNOLD SCHWARZENEGGER

We're often afraid of trying. What if we fail? Will others laugh at us? Will we feel stupid? Will we fall flat on our face?

Maybe. But, what will happen if we don't try? Will we be exactly at the same place we are now? Probably not. We'll be further back than we are now. Because, we'll have lost even more confidence in ourselves than we had to begin with. We'll know that we didn't have the courage to step up to the plate and take a swing at the ball. It doesn't matter if we get a strike. It matters that we are trying. Because one of these times, we will hit the ball.

That's how it is in recovery. We made the first big step when we said to ourselves that compulsive gambling wasn't working for us and we wanted to try recovery. So, we did. And, in working our program, we continue to try to take steps. Sometimes, we can make it only a half a step. Sometimes, we can only manage to stay where we are for today. That's o.k.

Today I will try to move forward in my program.
Forward in recovery.

June 17

There are no shortcuts to any place worth going.
ANONYMOUS

"I want to be recovered. When will it happen?" asks Mark. "Then, I can be done with this stuff. These meetings and groups and readings and staying away from gambling. When I'm recovered, I can just live my life without doing all of this."

The fact is recovery is our life if we are truly committed to living a life free from compulsive gambling. Everything we do revolves around staying clean. Recovery isn't taking a class or attending meetings for a few months and then being "cured." Without the support of our program, our gambling addiction can creep back into our lives like a cancer. Without our program, we start behaving the way we used to, a little at a time. We start lying again. We start covering our tracks, so others won't know we're slipping. We begin missing work. We slip in paying our bills. And, the vicious cycle of gambling starts again. So does the pain.

Recovery is important to us. Each action we take to keep our life free from gambling is vital to our success. Crucial to our peace and serenity. Thinking about it in terms of forever can be overwhelming. That's why we think of it in terms of today. Because all our today's turn into forever a day at a time.

I will remember that my recovery
is important each and every day.

June 18

Never continue in a job you don't enjoy. If you're happy in what you're doing, you'll like yourself, you'll have inner peace. And if you have that, along with physical health, you will have had more success than you could possibly have imagined."

JOHNNY CARSON

For so long, we've known the ultimate unhappiness. Our gambling certainly reinforced that. We struggled on a daily basis to keep up our addiction. It was a high maintenance situation and one that we couldn't control. In fact, it controlled us.

Now, we've found happiness in our recovery program. Each time we take a step forward in recovery, we find the peace we've been missing for so long. We understand that working our program brings us the success we want. It is the kind of success gambling couldn't provide for us. Our success in recovery means that serenity is ours. All we have to do is surrender our will to our Higher Power and seek assistance in walking the path of recovery.

~

I know that happiness and inner peace are mine in recovery.
I know I am successful working my program.

June 19

The only reactionaries are those who find themselves at home in the present.
NGGUEL DE UNAMUNO

For every action there is a reaction. We cannot control the actions others take. We can control our reactions to them, though.

Let's say someone starts yelling at us without giving us a chance to speak. We have some options. We can join them in a full-fledged screaming match to show them we can yell, too. Or, we can take another, calmer approach. We can tell the person in a quiet voice that we're willing to discuss the problem with them, but nothing can be accomplished when they are so upset. We can agree to meet with them again when they have a chance to calm down.

Both these options, and others, are available to us. It is our decision on which way we will react.

~

I will look for opportunities to react to
negative situations in an appropriate manner.
I will not get caught up in reacting negatively, too.

June 20

Sadness flies on the wings of the morning
and out of the heart of darkness comes the light.
THOMAS FULLER, M.D.

When we think of someone with depression, we usually think of a person curled up in bed, shades drawn and unable to make any effort to eat, get cleaned up or otherwise take care of themselves.

This isn't necessarily so. Terry is someone we would consider functionally depressed. Terry gets up every day, gets cleaned up and goes to work. She is doing her job and no more. But, Terry isn't really taking care of herself or her responsibilities like keeping her apartment clean, paying her bills or eating properly. She can't. It takes all her energy just to keep going in the limited manner she currently does.

Terry needs help. So do many of us. We need to look at ourselves and recognize the warning signs. Are we eating properly? Are we merely functioning at a minimal level in order to just get through the day?

There is nothing wrong with asking for assistance for our depression. There is a whole life wrong—ours—if we don't get help.

~

I will look at my life and see if I can identify
any warning signs of depression. I will seek help.

June 21

We probably have a greater love for those we support than those who support us.

ERIC HOFFER

Public television offers us many informative and educational programs. Viewers typically find them interesting, too. Public television is able to keep their programming more pure in terms of commercialism because they do not have endless advertisements interrupting the shows.

Public television depends on sponsors. Sponsorship is important to public television because it allows support in reaching the goals of the station without compromising the format of the programming.

We depend on sponsors in our program, too. And like public television, we are fortunate to be able to reach our goals of serenity with the loving support of our sponsors. They help us in our effort without compromising the integrity of our personal recovery program.

I have a strong support system in recovery.
I can work my program with their help.

June 22

He who limps is still walking.

STANISLAW LEE

Over the years, furniture can start to show wear and tear. What starts as a shiny new table can look weathered with years of use. After a while, nicks and dents begin to appear on the legs. The top may show a water ring or cigarette burn marks from displays of carelessness by the table's owners or guests.

The point is, it took several years to turn that brand new, unblemished table into a worn, rugged looking piece of used furniture. And like that battered table, it took many years of repeated nicks at our self-esteem to bring us to the point where we virtually had none.

In recovery, we are changing that, though. By removing the marks left by years of battering in our lives. Working our program helps us to fill in the nicks with peace of mind.

~

I am smoothing out the nicks in my life.
I am rebuilding my self-esteem.

June 23

There is no beauty like that which was spoiled by an accident, no accomplishments and graces are so to be envied as those that circumstances rudely hindered the development of.

CHARLES DUDLEY WARNER

Ralph worked hard on building a new closet for his bedroom. He painstakingly measured, put up studs, added sheet rock and smoothed drywall compound over the newly built walls. Next, Ralph sanded his work, preparing it for the new coat of paint.

The paint is on. In fact, the closet was painted three months ago. But, there the work stopped. The doors have yet to be hung and the trim work is still waiting to be finished.

What unfinished business do we have waiting for us today? Have we started our recovery program, only to stop, thinking we are cured and no longer need to take more steps?

~

I will examine my life for unfinished business.
I will make sure I am progressing
in my recovery program.

June 24

And men must walk, at least, before they dance.

ALEXANDER POPE

Bad means can't have good ends. Our goal is to remain clean from our addiction to gambling. How we meet that goal depends on the steps we take. Are we talking recovery, but not walking recovery. Have we become experts in preaching all the recovery lingo, but refuse to live it on a daily basis?

Words are helpful, but they are just words. To grow in recovery, we need to act. Every day. One day at a time. One step at a time. But, we do need to walk our talk.

~

I will not get caught up in becoming
a word expert in recovery. I will focus
my actions on my own program
and walk my recovery.

June 25

To deny all is to confess all.
SPANISH PROVERB

One of the worst feelings for us as a gambler was to admit we were helpless in our addiction. An early decision in our program was losing control of our money. We knew in order to move forward in recovery we must turn the responsibility for our money over to someone else.

Relinquishing control was tough. Because we were used to trying to control everyone and everything in our lives. Giving up control was an important step in our lives. And in our recovery. We know it's crucial to stop trying to control. After a while, we'll be in charge of our finances again. For now, though, we're working on being in charge of our lives.

I know the assistance I get in managing my money will help me in getting my life going in the right direction.

June 26

Instant gratification takes too long.

CARRIE FISHER

"I am so frustrated," pouted Kari, "I've been abstaining from gambling for two months now. How come I still have problems? Why isn't my life wildly happy?"

Many of us want instant recovery. We've hurt for so long that we want that pill or word or action that will make everything better. We want that to be able to live each day without any stress or problems to face.

Recovery doesn't mean we will never have stress again. It doesn't mean that all our problems will magically disappear. What recovery does mean is that we will have less stress and fewer problems. That will happen because we will make better decisions that will keep us from riding that chaotic roller coaster of emotions that get us into trouble. By working our program, we are ensured that we'll be able to handle the problems that we do face much better because we have built a foundation of peace. We are done creating problems for ourselves with our addictive behavior.

~

I know working my program will help me deal
with any problems that I have. I turn my will
over to my Higher Power for guidance.

June 27

You always pass failure on the way to success.

MICKEY ROONEY

We think we have to be perfect. Whenever we make a mistake, we don't even wait for others to comment. Instead, we're right in there, beating ourselves up for not being perfect. In the process, we judge others, putting our perfection expectations on them, too.

We've all failed at something. Actually, we've all failed at many things. Life isn't perfect. It can't be. Perfection puts too many stresses on us. It creates problems we don't need and can't manage.

Failure isn't important. It is what we do with those experiences. Do we berate ourselves and refuse to go on? Or, do we pick ourselves up and move on? Do we reject punishing ourselves because we know we are honestly doing our best? Even when we work our program with integrity, we will occasionally stumble. That is ok. What we do with that situation is what is important. Each time we stumble we are learning that perfection is not expected. What is expected is that we get right back on that path of recovery.

~

I will not judge myself or others.
I will expect integrity from myself, not perfection.

June 28

They always say that time changes things,
but you actually have to change them yourself.
ANDY WARHOL

Recovery is one place we can't ride on the coattails of others. We may have been able to slide through other situations in life by lining up with those doing the work. Recovery doesn't provide us that opportunity. We have to do the work ourselves.

Our recovery program is just that. Ours. It doesn't belong to anyone else. It isn't their responsibility, it is ours. Others may have experienced the same problems and pain as we have, but they cannot work through it for us. We are accountable for facing our issues head on. It is only by doing our own work that we can ease our suffering. We find our own serenity.

Others will always be there to support our efforts. They will want us to succeed as much as we want success for them. It is the support for each other that will encourage us all to commit to working our individual programs. For it is only in doing so that we can find true inner peace.

~

I take responsibility for working my own program.
I will accept the support of others, but I know
I must do my own work.

June 29

One of the most valuable things I've learned from archery is you can't do it well without believing in yourself.

GEENA DAVIS

"For so long, no one believed in me," said Sara. "I really couldn't blame them. I've told so many lies and failed on so many commitments. When I finally started telling the truth, I expected others to believe me. But, why would they? My track record with them hasn't been so great."

Sara is facing an issue we all face. While actively gambling, we couldn't be truthful. Being truthful meant we would have to face our gambling addiction. We'd also have to face the pain we'd lived with for so long. It was truly unbearable.

Entering recovery, we made our first and most important commitment. We turned our life over to our Higher Power. Secondly, we committed to being honest. Part of being honest means being truthful with ourselves and others. For most of us, this is the first time we have behaved this way.

We must remember, though, that others are more familiar with the behaviors we are getting rid of. They've lived with us lying for so long, it is hard to get them to believe us. We shouldn't get discouraged. It is important for us to keep telling the truth and keep behaving honestly. After a while, people will know that when we say something, they can believe us. And, they will!

~

I will tell the truth. Today and always.

June 30

Courage is the thing. All goes if courage goes.

J. M. BARRIE

Recovery is not a piece of cake. It does not just fall into our lives and suddenly cure us, making us forever happy. It takes work, at times a lot of work.

But, it goes beyond working our program. It requires courage. Courage to face our issues. Courage to stay with our personal recovery program when it seems to be a major struggle. Courage to stand up to those around us who are uncomfortable with our victory over compulsive gambling. Courage to just keep moving ahead.

So, we must stop from time to time and just think about the courage we have shown. We have to acknowledge the courage we have to draw upon at time to ensure we continue to live a life free from addiction.

~

I have the courage to work my program.
I have the courage to move forward
in my personal recovery.

July 1

And men must walk, at least, before they dance.
ALEXANDER POPE

Bad means can't have good ends. Our goal is to remain clean from our addiction to gambling. How we meet that goal depends on the steps we take. Are we talking recovery, but not walking recovery. Have we become experts in preaching all the recovery lingo, but refuse to live it on a daily basis?

Words are helpful, but they are just words. To grow in recovery, we need to act. Every day. One day at a time. One step at a time. But, we do need to walk our talk.

I will not get caught up in becoming a word expert in recovery. I will focus my actions on my own program and walk my recovery.

July 2

Today's preparation determines tomorrows achievement.

SAYING ON A PLAQUE

One day at a time. This is how we handle our recovery. Each day we lay more groundwork for continuing on in our program of tranquility.

It is important to take a step each day. Maybe today we feel we can't make huge strides. Rather, we are able to only take a baby step. Or maybe we feel we are crawling.

That's ok Because every movement we make forward in recovery helps us achieve our goal of maintaining serenity in our lives.

~

I will acknowledge my progress in recovery.
I know each tiny step I take keeps me free from gambling.

July 3

Jump for my love.
POINTER SISTERS

The rules always changed for Jean. As a child, she tried so hard to please her parents. But no matter what Jean did, it was never enough. She made straight A's in school, played in the band, was captain of the soccer team. But, her parents frequently reminded her she didn't measure up to their standards. Jean never felt she could earn their love.

No one needs to jump through hoops to deserve another's love. We've been down that road. It doesn't work.

Love is unconditional. Love is accepting. Love is respectful.

~

I love myself. I accept who I am.
I am a beautiful, loving human being.

July 4

Admitted to ourselves and to another human being the exact nature of our wrongs.

STEP 5

This steps allows us to let go of our guilt. It's not an easy step because our ego can get in the way of admitting our wrongs to someone else.

But, in order to be successful, we must push our ego aside and face ourselves head on, right down to our soul.

What a cleansing feeling we experience in this step. Remember impression without expression leads to depression.

~

I will push my ego out of the way and take part
in the purging of my wrongs and guilt.
I will cleanse my soul.

July 5

She makes me so angry.

JOE

No one can tell us how to feel. Our feelings are ours. We need to own them. We need to take responsibilities for our feelings.

So, in Joe's case, she—whoever she is—can't make Joe feel anything. Joe must take accountability for how he feels. He feels angry. And, that's o.k.

I will remember that I am the owner of my feelings.
I will feel my feelings.

July 6

Let Go and Let God.

We have been practicing our unhealthy behaviors for so long, that it is hard to make them just disappear. No one expects us to. What our recovery process teaches us is that we need to work at ridding ourselves of these negative actions a step at a time. A day at a time.

Think of it this way. Imagine being on your feet all day. Your feet are killing you. You are in a great deal of pain. So the minute you walk in the door at home, you kick off your shoes. How do your feet feel now?

Relieved. Just like ridding ourselves of our destructive behavior.

~

I am thankful to be releasing myself
from the unhealthy behaviors of compulsive gambling.

July 7

There's a spirit that guides me, a light that shines for me.
My life is worth livin', I don't need to see the end.
JOHN DENVER, "SWEET SURRENDER"

Compulsive gambling brought us to the brink of suicide. We could not see any way out. The big dark hole seemed the only escape.

We gave up hope. But, it didn't give up on us. Each of us has a story to tell on how we survived.

The important thing is we did survive. We were given a chance to live our lives—in recovery. Today I am the architect of my life.

I will remember how precious life is to me.
I know my life—in recovery—is worth living.
I am happy to be alive.

July 8

Remember to exercise.

COVERT BAILEY

Everything around us is health, wellness, exercise. Aerobics today. Racquetball tomorrow.

Our health is important. But, it is not necessary to be a fitness freak in order to be healthy. In fact, becoming a fitness freak can be unhealthy for us if we are approaching it in a compulsive manner.

Health means taking care of ourselves. Eating right. Exercising properly. Staying clean. Staying serene.

~

I know that being healthy
means taking good care of my health
my body, my mind and my spirituality.

July 9

Let go of your judgments to see beyond the illusions.
SANAYA ROMAN

Joe thinks that Jackie is unfriendly. "I smiled across the room at her at a meeting, but she just looked away and started talking towards another small group of people. She is really conceited."

Joe quickly jumped to the conclusion that Jackie was vain because she didn't easily return his friendliness. He didn't stop to think that perhaps this was Jackie's first meeting. She may be scared. She may be shy. And maybe the reason she quickly headed for the group was that she needed to feel safe; perhaps her sponsor was standing with those people.

We need to make sure we don't put our beliefs onto others' actions. Before reacting, we must stop to think about others, not just ourselves. We must be careful not to judge the actions of others. After all, we're asking them not to judge us.

~

I will take care in putting my judgments on others' behaviors. I will remember that others may be in difficult places in their lives, too.

July 10

Learn to receive all the good things your higher self has to give you.

SANAYA ROMAN

In recovery, we turn our lives and will over to our Higher Power. At times, especially early in our recovery program, we may struggle with letting go completely and try taking back some of the control We wrestle with trusting another to help us straighten out our lives.

What is important for us to remember at these times is that we tried it our way and it didn't work. When we were "in control" of our lives, we were caught up in our gambling addiction.

We deserve what the good life has to offer. That good comes through trusting our Higher Power to guide us in our recovery from chaos and into serenity.

~

The guidance from my Higher Power
is crucial to my recovery. I am open
to receiving the good, the serenity offered.

July 11

Solitude vivifies; isolation kills.

JOSEPH ROUX

The more we sunk into the disease of compulsive gambling, the more isolated we became. We knew if we kept to ourselves, we would keep others from seeing what was happening to us.

In isolation, we looked at reality through our eyes only. We denied that there was any other reality and we denied we were in trouble. Isolation kept us safe from true reality and stuck in our sickness.

We have since learned that true reality is recovery. By breaking out of our isolation we can focus on the world around us. While working our program, we can also care about others.

~

No longer do I isolate myself from
the world around me. I am in touch with true reality.

July 12

Can man change? His memories are only from his childhood . . .
it is memory that conditions and shapes responses to life
and determines patterns of growth.

JOSHUA

Change is important to our recovery. Memories from our childhood show that a lot of our gambling behaviors are deep rooted as a result of our childhood experiences. We grew up with low self-esteem and loneliness through our emotional isolation from the world.

In recovery, we take a strong look at what we came to believe about ourselves in childhood . More importantly, we begin to break down the myth that we are bad people, unworthy of anything. We see that we do have worth and our personal boundaries are important. We begin to live our lives, not the lives we were told how to live. Change for us means growth.

~

I am changing the beliefs I had about myself.
The old beliefs were based on others' words.
My new beliefs are based on my truths.

July 13

Impression without expression leads to depression.

PHIL HANSON

Many events leave impressions on our lives. When someone treats us cruelly, we may be angry. Or a friend may do something that hurts our feelings. The death of someone important to use can leave us feeling sad.

How do we express our feelings of anger, hurt or sadness? Maybe the bigger question is to take a step back and ask do we express our feelings?

Leaving feelings unexpressed can cause us to internalize them. As feeling after feeling builds up in us with no release, we can become more and more hopeless. Hopelessness leads to depression.

~

It is important for me to express my feelings.
I will release them in a letter or verbally
with a trusted support person.

July 14

There is no such thing as girl feelings or boy feelings.
There are only feelings.
MIKE MARCOTTE

As people begin to get in touch with their feelings in recovery, they'll often say such things as "I was taught boys don't cry. To me, that means sadness is a girl feeling." Or a woman may share, "I was told I could not get angry because it wasn't ladylike."

The simple truth is feelings don't have gender. Men and boys feel sad just like females. Women and girls get angry just like males. The range of feelings is open to everyone, regardless of their sex. It is up to us, as a person—not a male or female—to decide how we feel.

~

My feelings, whatever they may be, are right for me.
I will not allow others to determine my feelings.

July 15

A universal feeling, whether will or ill founded,
cannot be safely disregarded.
ABRAHAM LINCOLN

Growing up in a dysfunctional family system, we learned to hide our feelings. Whenever we attempted to feel them, we were told were stupid or a baby or something similar. Or maybe we were physically punished. Emotions weren't allowed.

No wonder we struggle with our feelings now. We try to identify and experience them. We know that's the way we get in touch with them. But, it's pretty scary for us. Emotions surface that we've never dealt with before.

As we grow in recovery, we know feeling our feelings will become less scary and more natural. We know getting in touch with our feelings is healthy progress in recovery.

~

Although I may be afraid of my emotions
as they surface, I know I am taking steps
forward in recovery.

July 16

Those people who are uncomfortable in themselves
are disagreeable to others.
WILLIAM HAZLITT

As we move forward in recovery, our emerging self begins to surface. This can be an uneasy process for us because we naturally fear what is unfamiliar to us. What will we uncover? Who will we find inside? Will we be the same person we were?

We need to trust that our emerging self in recovery will be a healthier self. Sure, we've displayed some inappropriate behavior while gambling. Yes, we've made some poor decisions. But, we aren't bad people. Recovery shows us this. It shows us, too, how to build on each step of progress we make in our program.

~

I will greet my emerging self like a newfound friend.
I am curious about meeting the new me.

July 17

The barricade closes the street but opens the way.

GRAFFITI

During road construction, highway crews put up roadblocks. The roadblocks are used to protect motorists from driving in unsafe areas or even off a bridge.

In recovery, we need to put up our own roadblocks. They will protect us from slipping off the road of recovery and into the ditch of compulsive gambling. Our personal roadblocks may include leaving our checkbook in the care of a trusted supporter of our efforts to remain clean. That way, the enticement to detour won't be strong. Personal roadblocks will keep us on the road to recovery.

~

I will look at my personal recovery program
to see where I can put up roadblocks to help me.
I will not be detoured by temptation.

July 18

I don't think I'm a compulsive gambler.
I only gambled for six months. I haven't been doing this very long.

MIKE

What Mike doesn't realize, because he's actively in denial, is that it's not the frequency of gambling that's important. In Mike's very short (to him) months of gambling, he still told lies, still broke promises, and still stole money from his employer. All in an attempt to experience the excitement of the high.

We can't compare ourselves to other compulsive gamblers and rationalize away our addiction. No matter what the length of time, the bottom line is that compulsive gambling had a hold on us. It made our lives unmanageable.

~

I won't get caught up in addiction comparisons.
I am a compulsive gambler and I am
working my recovery program.

July 19

A borrowed cloak does not keep one warm.
ARABIC PROVERB

One of our gambling behaviors was to "borrow against our win." Typically, we would borrow money from a friend, family member, credit card or maybe even resorted to stealing. Our intentions were to pay it back when we hit a big win.

We also "borrowed against our life" while gambling. We lived our lives in a vicious circle. Our health suffered, our spirituality suffered, our mental well-being suffered. We were using a our physical, spiritual and mental strength just to survive. But, we found out we couldn't.

We're surviving in recovery. In fact, we're thriving. No more borrowing against our lives. We're living them now in the present.

~

Recovery is my key to life.
No more borrowing for me.

July 20

Our natural egoism leads us to judge people
by their relations to ourselves.
W. SOMERSET MAUGHAM

Ego means many things. Before recovery, one meaning it had for us was Edging God Out. We didn't want our Higher Power in our lives because we didn't want any being to know how we were behaving. We were not proud of our preoccupation with gambling, but we seemed helpless to stop.

Our lives were spiritually empty. Until that day we admitted our lives were out of control and we couldn't go on as an active gambler. At that point, we stopped edging God out and began letting our Higher Power in.

Ego to me in recovery means
Every Good Opportunity to
work my program and live in serenity.

July 21

Happiness is beneficial for the body . . . .

MARCEL PROUST

Gambling was an attempt to disassociate from our feelings. We figured we could distract ourselves from facing our issues.

Happiness didn't come. Instead, we suffered more. Gambling only added to our problems, compounding our pain to the point where our lives became totally unbearable.

Happiness is attainable for us in recovery. Removing our addictions and working our program allows us to find the peace and serenity we want and deserve.

~

Happiness is available in recovery.
I do not need the distractions of addiction.

July 22

Pain makes man think.
Thought makes man wise.
Wisdom makes life endurable.
JOHN PATRICK

Before recovery, we used many alternatives to deal with our pain. These methods usually turned our feelings in on ourselves. Those feelings, however, worked their way to the surface and came out in many ways at the worst times. Sometimes we displayed our conduct disorder by physically fighting—in school, in a bar, or maybe at a party. Or maybe we became so overly sensitive that we continually misinterpreted every comment or action and felt others were always against us.

We need to face our feelings head on. And learn to deal with them in healthy way. It ensures that we act appropriately in releasing those feelings and spare us—and others—from inappropriate and destructive behaviors.

~

I will work on experiencing my feelings in healthy ways and working through them in non-destructive manners.

July 23

For fate has wove the thread of life with pain . . .

HOMER

Post traumatic stress is commonly thought to be a result of participating in a war. Most of us are familiar with the fact that a lot of Viet Nam veterans have been diagnosed with this disorder.

Many gamblers suffer this affliction without understanding it. The battle for them may be abuse, incest, death of someone important to them or another equally significant traumatic event.

In order to avoid the pain, we took ourselves out of reality and into the fantasy world of gambling. We are addressing our gambling compulsive gambling in recovery. We also need to make sure we identify our pain and work through it.

~

I will make every effort to identify my issues
and to work through my pain.

July 24

Habit, a shackle for the free.

AMBROSE PIERCE

Is compulsive gambling the single addiction in our lives? Is it the only area where our lives have become unmanageable? Or are there others?

Are we working on freedom from gambling while we continue to actively practice co-dependency? Are we so wrapped up in another person that our identity is given over to that person and relationship?

Peace and serenity are ours. But in order to truly experience this ultimate joy, we must free our lives from all addictions. To be truly free in recovery, we must be totally free of addictions.

~

I want release from all my addictions.
I want freedom in recovery.

July 25

Were entirely ready to have these defects of character removed.

STEP 6

What are our flaws? Grandiosity? Lying? Anger? Impatience? Hatred? Fear?

After we've identified them for ourselves, how do we get rid of them? No, they won't just vanish. We have to work to get rid of them, that's for sure.

We need to blot them out one by one. A bit at a time. We must prepare ourselves—mind, body and spirit. We must open ourselves to release all these self defeating behaviors and emotions.

~

I will work on removing my character flaws
one at a time, making another step forward
in my recovery program of piece.

July 26

Happy recovery to me, happy recovery to me,
happy recovery dear Alicia, happy recovery to me.

ALICIA J.

Some of us will be celebrating an annual anniversary today. Our anniversary will mark the number of years we have abstained from compulsive gambling. From all of our partners in recovery, we are hearing CONGRATULATIONS!

There are many who may not be hitting an annual anniversary today, but they should also be acknowledged. Some have completed one day, one week or one month of abstinence from gambling. CONGRATULATIONS to you, too. Because each day, week, month or year we abstain from gambling and work our personal recovery rewards us with serenity.

~

Congratulations to me for the work I am doing on my personal recovery journey.

July 27

Ill habits gather by unseen degrees—
as brooks make rivers, rivers run to seas.

OVID

Seldom does an addiction live in an empty house. In working our recovery program, we have identified compulsive gambling as a problem. But, are there other addictions in our lives that we are not addressing?

These additional addictions may exist in various areas of our life. Are we workaholics, devoting unrealistic time and energy to our jobs? Is alcohol a problem for us? Do we use food to bury our feelings and, hopefully, our pain?

~

Today I will take a look into other areas of my life.
I will seek help in removing all addictions from my life.

July 28

Noble deeds and not baths are the best cures for depression.

DODIE SMITH

Depression in today's society is like the common cold. No longer does it carry the stigma of being crazy or nuts. Society is more informed.

We know depression all too well. Our despondency prevented us from living normal lives. It helped lead us to gambling. But the gambling didn't help. The cloud of gloom continued to hover over us.

We can get help for our depression in recovery. We only need to ask for help. We need not be ashamed or afraid. There is hope.

I know help is available for depression.
I only need to ask for it.

July 29

Solitude is the mother of anxieties.
PUBLILIUS SYRUS

It is not uncommon for compulsive gamblers to be considered antisocial. We have learned to turn our feelings inside and we also master the ability to live our lives without letting others get close to us. Perhaps we had behavior problems in school. Or struggled to keep a job. Throughout life, our feelings continue to manifest themselves in destructive manners.

In recovery, we are learning to open up, to work our program with the support of others. We don't have to do this alone. We don't have to withdraw anymore. Help is available.

~

I am not alone in recovery.
I have support to work my program.

July 30

Seeing's believing, but feeling's the truth.

THOMAS FULLER, M.D.

We have struggled through life unable to express our feelings. Early in life, we learned some painful lessons when we tried to verbalize what was going on inside. We were not allowed to cry. Nor were we permitted to feel our sadness.

Later on, we turned to gambling. It gave us an opportunity to again avoid our pain. When we gambled, we could take ourselves out of reality and into a fantasy world.

Sooner or later, though, the fantasy ended and we had to face reality again. An reality didn't look good to us. That's why we choose recovery. Where we are learning to feel our feelings, to be ourselves. Recovery is our reality now.

~

I know my reality in recovery depends on facing my feelings. I will not use distractions to avoid reality.

July 31

The direct speech of feeling is allegorical and cannot be replaced by anything.

BORIS PASTERNAK

Sometimes our feelings take us by surprise. It could be that we are so unused to being able to express them that they scare us. Our feelings have been stuffed inside of us for so long that when they do start to surface they may come out in explosions, bubbling to the surface and spewing in all directions.

That is why it is so important for us to surround ourselves with people who understand. People who have been where we are. People who can help us safely feel our feelings.

~

I know it is important to get in touch with my feelings.
I will allow my friends in recovery
to help me in this effort.

August 1

Perhaps even one's feelings get tired, when one is alone with oneself.

UGO BETTI

Compulsive gambles are loners. We know that. It could be we became so antisocial because of our treatment as a child. Many of us were continually forced to internalize our feelings because our parents did not allow us to display them. Maybe we were told we were wrong to express our feelings.

So, we kept to ourselves. Now in recovery, we are learning to come in touch with our feelings. We are giving ourselves permission to feel. Along with this, we are beginning to come out of our shell.

~

It is important for me to identify with my feelings.
I know in doing so, I am becoming more social.

August 2

Every path has its puddle.
ENGLISH PROVERB

Bill was a jogger who ran the same route every day. He started from his house, wound around the park a mile away and always ended up at his neighbor's house. At this house he always chatted with his best friend while he cooled down after his run.

After two years, Bill's friend and neighbor sold his house. Bill still jogged his normal path, but something didn't feel as good. It took him a while to figure it out, but then realized what was missing was his best friend when he stopped at the end of his run. Bill then knew the source of his loss.

Sometimes, we continue in old patterns because they are familiar to us. Even if they aren't healthy for us, we hesitate to change because we don't know what the changes will bring. In recovery, we can be assured they will bring us continued growth and serenity.

~

I will examine the patterns in my life. I need not fear change if it results in growth in recovery.

August 3

We are shrubs, planted in a new place,
needing care and water to grow again.
TRAN VAN HUNG

All human beings need nurturing. We, as recovering adults, are no exception. Most of us have had limited or no nurturing in our lives. That's what helped lead us into our addiction.

Recovery allows us to get some of the nurturing needs we have met. Through others in recovery. But, most importantly, from ourselves. Because being involved in our personal recovery program means we take care of ourselves— our needs, our emotions, our feelings.

Nurturing ourselves allows us to grow. It allows us to see how valuable we are. It encourages us to continue in our program of personal recovery. And, it allows us to begin to nurture those around us without sacrificing ourselves.

~

I know that I have needs and feelings
that need nurturing. I will
be attentive to myself today.

August 4

It seemed to me that death would finally give me life.

JIM A.

Sinking into the depths of depression is an overwhelming feeling. We feel that there is no way we can pick ourselves up; no one who can help us; and no means to remove the problems from our lives. Maybe our emptiness has been so deep, we have considered ending our life.

Depression does not mean the end. We can get help. The help can show us how to move out of our despair. With the support of our recovery program, we can pull ourselves out of the darkness and into the light of life.

~

In recovery, there is help for depression.
No one needs to live in the shadows of gloom.
The sunlight of life is ours.

August 5

We didn't all come over in the same ship, but we're all in the same boat.

SAYING ON A PLAQUE

We met our bottom through different forms of gambling. Some of us played slots. Others were addicted to bingo or horses or pull tabs.

It doesn't really matter what our game of choice was, how we found our action or how we chased our losses. For each of us, it had the same result disaster.

How wonderful, though, that we have jumped the compulsive gambling ship and boarded the boat sailing in the waters of recovery.

~

I am thankful to be on board with shipmates who are sailing forward with me in recovery.

August 6

Golf without bunkers and hazards
would be tame and monotonous. So would life.

B. C. FORBES

Sometimes it seems like one obstacle after another is placed in our path. Is this what recovery is all about? We thought recovery was an easing of troubles, not an addition of more.

But, if we take a minute to think back, we will remember that our troubles were worse and more abundant during our active compulsive gambling days. How did we deal with them at that time? Mostly by denying there was a problem. Maybe we threw the overdue bills away so we wouldn't be reminded of them. Maybe we didn't answer the phone.

Recovery never promised no troubles. It does promise the ability to deal with those problems in a rational, peaceful way. Recovery can't make all troubles go away. But, it can help us grow by showing us we can handle our problems.

~

I will remember that challenges will always be part of my life. That's the real world. But, I know I can handle my problems and continue on my personal recovery program of peace and serenity.

August 7

. . . our happiness hinges not on good luck; it hinges on peace of heart.

DAVID STEINDL-RAST

We've played the game of luck thousands of times. It seemed that the more luck was against us, the more involved we would be in our gambling addiction. That's because we "knew" that any moment our luck would change and we would begin "coming back."

While we were focusing on our luck, we forfeited our peace and serenity. Instead, we were caught up in the frenzy of our addiction. But, our luck ran out.

Now, in our personal recovery, we have released that frenzy. We have given up focusing on the luck of the win and are giving our attention to our happiness. We have found out, and we continue to experience, that the real luck for us has been our decision to work our personal recovery program. A program that lets us find happiness and serenity on a daily basis.

~

I am thankful that I am finding peace and serenity in my personal recovery program. I know that happiness is based on my involvement in recovery.

August 8

The will to win is not nearly as important as the will to prepare to win.
BOBBY KNIGHT

How many times have we worried about how a situation will turn out? We play it over again and again in our minds, causing great worry and frustration. At times, we even make ourselves sick. Or figure, what's the use?

This kind of thinking can bring us dangerously close to slipping back into our active addiction. But, how do we combat it?

By remembering that we are not in control of outcomes. What we are in control of is the process. As long as we take the steps necessary to accomplish something, that's all we can ask of ourselves. If we have given a situation our best shot, then we can be proud of ourselves.

It's not important that we win. It is important that we play the game.

~

Today I will be actively involved in my process.
I will let go of the outcome
and know that I have given my best.

August 9

Once, when I was little, I asked a neighbor lady
for an ice cream cone when we went to the store together.
When my mother found out, she spanked me, put me in my room
and told me never to ask for things again.

ANN J.

Many of us have trouble asking for what we need. It's because as children we were taught that it is bad to ask for things. That it was bad manners and if we displayed bad manners, it meant we were bad. The punishment of being struck or placed in solitude was not nearly as devastating as the message that we were bad.

As adults, we have carried that message with us. We have trouble asking for what we need because we received messages over and over again that we are not allowed to do so. Instead, we either assume others should know what we need, or we just stuff our needs.

Needs don't get met that way. We know that first hand. After years of not getting our needs met, we need to let them be known. No, we don't run around telling others what they must do for us. But, we do have to say what we need when we need it.

~

I know that my needs are important.
I will let my needs be known.

August 10

Today's preparation determines tomorrows achievement.

SAYING ON A PLAQUE

One day at a time. This is how we handle our recovery. Each day we lay more groundwork for continuing on in our program of tranquility.

It is important to take a step each day. Maybe today we feel we can't make huge strides. Rather, we are able to only take a baby step. Or maybe we feel we are crawling.

That's o.k. Because every movement we make forward in recovery helps us achieve our goal of maintaining serenity in our lives.

~

I will acknowledge my progress in recovery. I know each tiny step I take keeps me free from gambling.

August 11

A bad habit never disappears miraculously;
it's an undo-it-yourself project.
ABIGAIL VAN BUREN

Why do we feel it's necessary to lie? Is it because we think the truth isn't enough? Maybe we think others who we feel are important in our lives will find us lacking because our truth isn't grandiose or noteworthy.

Lying gets us nowhere. It destroys our self-esteem. It says to others and ourselves that we don't think a lot about ourselves and our self-respect.

We can't guarantee the truth will be enough for anyone else. But, it can be enough for us. By telling the truth, we say we respect who we are; what our values are. Telling the truth, no matter how uneventful it may seem, allows us to be us. For in telling the truth, we are saying to ourselves "I am good enough."

Today I will look myself in the mirror and say,
"I am more than good enough.
I am a beautiful human being of this earth."
I will affirm my self-respect.

August 12

If you don't have all the things you want,
be grateful for all the things you don't have that you didn't want.
THOMAS JEFFERSON

We always want more. That's human nature. More money. More cars. More vacations. More clothes. The list goes on and on.

Does recovery mean less? It sure does! Less compulsion. Less excuses for our behavior. Less anxiety. Less lying. Less shame. Less anger. Less distrust, fear and resentment. This list goes on and on, too.

Recovery means more, too. More serenity. More peace. More joy. More happiness. More sanity.

Recovery means more to me.
More promise for a life full of
all the good this world has to offer.

August 13

Being fat doesn't mean you feel good about yourself, but neither does being skinny.

ROSANNE BARR

Nowadays, there are numerous ads in newspapers and magazines for beauty shots. "Let us make you over." "Look like a model." "Wear professional makeup, hair and clothing." "Give that someone special a glamour photo of you."

But, once the glamour is removed, what will we find in the mirror? Once we take off the professional makeup, who will we see?

Its great to have fun with glamour photos. But, when our moment of glamour is gone and we go back to being who we are, we need to be at peace with who we find. Glamour is ours for an instant. Beauty from within is ours forever.

~

Today, I will look at myself in the mirror and say
"You are truly a beautiful creation of the earth."
I am pleased that my beauty is internal
and brings be peace and joy in my recovery.

August 14

We are what we repeatedly do.
Excellence, then is not an act,
but a habit.
ARISTOTLE

What does out behavior tell others? Are we speaking the words of recovery, but walking the road of compulsive gambling? Are we telling others one thing, but doing another?

Recovery means walking the walk. The words of recovery are great. But the recovery behavior needs to back up those words. Recovery behavior may not be easy for us. Especially in the beginning of our recovery program. But, it's important to keep our recovery behavior in line. So we can "talk the talk" and "walk the walk." That's recovery.

I will remember that my actions
speak louder than words. I will show myself
that my recovery behavior is working for me.
Then, others will see it, too.

August 15

God takes us where we can grow the most.

JUDY L.

Sometimes it seems like God (or our Higher Power as we describe it) constantly tests us. One thing after another goes "wrong." We aren't invited to an event that is really important to us. A family member comes down with a serious illness. We lose our job due to a layoff.

At times like these we may want to say, "O.k., God, I know what you're up to. I can't pass your tests. Just give me an "F" and leave me alone."

We have to remember, though, that we tried it alone. And it didn't work for us. That's why we "Came to believe that a Power greater than ourselves could restore us to sanity." Our Power isn't giving us "tests." Our Power is helping us learn the lessons we need to stay on the track of recovery.

~

Today I will look inside the challenges
in my path of recovery and know
there is a new source of strength to be uncovered.

August 16

People can be divided into three groups:
those who make things happen,
those who watch things happen and
those who wonder what happened.
Showing up is 80% of life.

WOODY ALLEN

Sometimes it's hard to show up for a meeting. We may be discouraged because recovery isn't going as quickly as we want it to. So, why show up? We think it's never going to work.

"Bring the body and the mind will follow" is a potent recovery phrase. At times, just showing up for a meeting is the absolute best we can do for that day. But, that's o.k. In fact, that's wonderful.

Why? Because we made a decision to stick with our recovery program. Even through our rough spots. Because little steps showing up—are better than no steps at all.

I will remember that, although I may get discouraged
from time to time, recovery works.
It is my only hope for peace and serenity.

August 17

The real measure of your wealth is
how much you'd be worth if you lost all your money.
CHARLES DE GAULLE

Money can buy a lot of "things." Houses, fancy clothes, big cars, exotic vacations. Before recovery, we had a number of them. And lost them.

What was left underneath was a human being. A bit scared. With self-esteem at an all time low. But, with the smallest shred of hope.

Hope for a life that would bring happiness. We understood that we needed to work our program. But, we also came to know that "our program works." And, what we found was a beautiful person. With a lot to offer. Themselves—and others.

~

Today I will measure my worth by what I really have—serenity.

August 18

Obstacles are those frightful things you see
when you take your eyes off your goals.
SYDNEY SMITH

Recovery isn't a burden to bear. It's a joy to be lived. Sometimes we take our eyes off our daily goals of peace and serenity. When we do that, things can get pretty frightening.

We don't have to bite off recovery in one huge mouthful. That can be pretty overwhelming. Instead we can take it a tiny bite at a time. We can adjust our behavior for the next five minutes. We'll worry about the hours and the weeks later.

That doesn't mean "five minutes in recovery, then the rest of the day off." It means do what you can. Right now. Today. This minute.

Today I will remember that
although I will live my personal recovery program
the entire day, I can do it a minute at a time.

August 19

The graveyards are full of indispensable people."
CHARLES DE GAULLE

Did we trade one addiction for another. It's easy to do. Sure, we're not gambling. But, we may have become workaholics instead. Working day and night. Never having fun. In other words, we may be using another addiction as a way to keep us from gambling.

We know from our experiences that addictions and compulsions don't bring happiness. Abstinence does. Working our program does. Living our recovery does.

We need to participate in our program. Every day. Every hour. Every minute. A minute at a time may be all we can do. That's o.k. Because those minutes will eventually become hours. And the hours will become days. Days free from addiction. Days full of serenity.

~

Today, I will remember to work my recovery program
in little steps. I know it is better to be free
of compulsion in little steps than to trade
one addiction in for another just as damaging.

August 20

Peace is not something you wish for. It is something you make, something you do, something you are, and something you give away.

ROBERT FULGHUM

In recovery, we continue to make a life of peace and joy for ourselves. We tried living the other way, the compulsive gambling way—and it never worked for us. Recovery does.

Each day we live in our recovery program, it becomes who we are. We are peaceful, joyful and, most of all, serene. We are experiencing happiness; most of us for the first time. It feels great!

We give that same peace, joy and serenity to others in the way we act. No, we can't make others recover; we know everyone must do that for themselves. But as people watch us, they can see what the journey in recovery has given us; and can give them.

~

I will remember that not everyone is experiencing the serenity I have found in my recovery program. I am thankful for the peace and joy my program has given me.

August 21

Whoever gossips to you will gossip of you.

SPANISH PROVERB

It's easy to talk about someone else. "Look at them. Look at what they are doing wrong." Because if we focus on others 'problems, we don't have to face the reality of ours.

That's plain stinkin' thinkin'. We all have a past. But, for all the struggles we have had, we are still beautiful, wonderful human beings. We still have problems, but we have a lot more peace and joy than we did before beginning our recovery program.

So, let's take the focus off of gossiping about someone else. Instead, let's see the good in others—and ourselves. That's walking what we're talking.

I will remember that gossip serves no purpose,
except to hurt someone. I want others
to find the joy I have found.
I will walk what I talk.

August 22

Its never too late—never too late to start over, never too late to be happy.

JANE FONDA

You can't teach an old dog new tricks, the saying goes. Apparently, it's meant to tell us that once we reach a certain age, we are locked into our learned behaviors forever.

In recovery, we know that's not true. It doesn't matter if we are 15 or 25 or 55 or 75. We can change. We can learn new behaviors. It isn't easy, but if we stick with our program, we can find happiness.

Today I will remember that it doesn't matter how old I am. Each day I am learning something new. I am learning peace and happiness.

August 23

I'm always very relieved to be somebody else,
because I'm not sure at all who I am.

MAGGIE SMITH

In order to protect ourselves from harmful sun rays, we cover our bodies with sun lotions. Some block out the sun. Others let a few rays at us. Some don't screen out the sun at all.

In order to protect ourselves in life, we've covered ourselves with roles that screened out who we are in the hopes that we would be approved of. We used our gambling addiction to guard against anyone finding out we weren't perfect.

In recovery, we don't need to shelter who we are. We can open the door and let ourselves out. We don't need other's approval because we have approval from the best source possible—ourselves.

~

Today I approve of myself
and the progress I'm making.

August 24

Honesty is something you can't wear out.

WAYLON JENNINGS

In step 5 of our recovery program, we admit to ourselves and to another human being the exact nature of our wrongs. Because before we can be honest with others, we have to be honest with ourselves.

Its not necessary to beat ourselves up. We've made mistakes. We've taken part in some poor decisions. We've hurt others. And, we've hurt ourselves.

Getting honest allows us to acknowledge those errors in judgment. And learn from them. Honesty keeps us clean. Honesty keeps us free.

I will be honest with myself and others.
Honesty is the only way to go.

August 25

Life consists of merging and emerging relationships.

BILL D.

Friendships with others are an important part of life. Some of us are still friends with people we met in elementary school. And we've made friends along our life's way.

Like other relationships, friendships take work. They take giving. They take trust. For friends allow themselves to open up. To know each other, both the weaknesses and the strengths.

Friends don't need to be together all the time. Sometimes the best friendships are between people who only see each other a couple of times a year. But, each takes responsibility for caring for the relationship and sustaining it's commitment with each person as an individual and together as friends.

~

I know that friends are precious to my life.
I am committed to my responsibilities
in my relationships with my friends.

August 26

Love does not begin and end the way we seem to think it does;
Love is a battle, love is a war; love is a growing up.

JAMES BALDWIN

Love doesn't happen at "first sight." We may be attracted to someone because they are good looking, are witty or are interesting.

Real love goes beyond this. It allows us to reveal ourselves, the blemishes, quirks, and all, to our significant person. It allows us to be who we are. Real love understands that who we are is great.

Our significant other must also be willing to let us know them. In a real love relationship, the walls come down and the foundation of love is built together.

~

I know that love involves give and take.
It allows each of us to know and care for the other.

August 27

Life was not meant to be endured, but enjoyed.

HUBERT H. HUMPHREY

Life is beautiful. There are many things that we can be thankful for in our lives. A child's delightful laugh. A sailboat gracefully crossing the water. The sunset. Recovery.

For being in recovery has allowed us to discover the pleasures of life we may not have known existed. Recovery is happiness. Recovery is appreciating the good in our lives.

Today I will remember the good in my life.
I will enjoy the happiness recovery has given me.

August 28

Misery no longer loves company. Nowadays, it insists upon it.

RUSSELL BAKER

"They did it to me." "Why does this always happen to me?" "I never get anything." "He hurt my feelings." "My boss doesn't like me." "You don't understand."

Statements of victims. More likely than not, we've personally used a few of them. It's easy to buy into the victim mentality. Being a victim means someone else is responsible, not us. Taking responsibility means owning our feelings, our decisions and our actions. Undoing the chains that keep us in the victim role releases us from the burden of blame. Instead, we move towards the freedom of individuality.

I do not want to be a victim.
I am responsible for myself.
I am free from the burden of blame.

August 29

The most important thing a man has
to tell you is what he is not telling you.

LYNDON B. JOHNSON

Communication happens in many ways. Of course, we all know that people write and speak to communicate. But just as important is the ability to listen.

By listening to ourselves, for instance, we can identify how we feel about a person or situation. What are we hearing from within based on our feelings?

Secondly, we need to trust ourselves. Our feelings are signaling to us what is right and wrong for us. By listening to those feelings, we can deal with anything we come across.

~

Today I will listen to myself.
I will trust my feelings.

August 30

A child needs your love most when he deserves it least.

ERMA BOMBECK

Sometimes children have just plain naughty days. They spill their milk, pull the cat's tail and throw their ball down the toilet. And that's just during the first hour they are awake!

Children don't set out to misbehave. In their own way, they are trying to tell us that something isn't right in their world. Maybe they are hungry or tired. Maybe they are scared. Whatever is happening with them, they need our understanding.

It's the same for the child within us. Sometimes there are things going on within that we have trouble identifying. We need to be understanding with our child within.

~

I may not always be in touch with my inner child.
But, I will listen and try to understand.

August 31

Just as a baby learns to walk by falling down repeatedly, we must remember that we are babies in the new world.

SHAKTI GAWAIN

It's o.k. to make mistakes. Even in recovery, we stumble now and then. It may not be a step back into compulsive gambling. It may be an error in judgment or some misspoken words.

Perfection isn't promised in recovery. What does happen, however, is that by following our program we learn how to quickly recognize our mistakes and get back on the recovery road.

Today I will recognize my mistakes and
grow stronger in my recovery by working my program.

September 1

The world knows no less rational person than a losing bettor.

PETE ROZELLE

Gambling addiction brings craziness. The more we tried to control our lives through gambling, the more unmanageable they became.

Desperation brought us into our recovery program. And, as we began to work with the program and release our need for compulsive gambling, we found sanity in our lives. For many of us, this was the first time we had done so.

Moving forward in recovery tiny step by tiny step allows us to build a solid base for continued growth and joy in our lives.

I am thankful my recovery program
helped me find sanity in my life.

September 2

For I don't care too much for money,
For money can't buy me love.
JOHN LENNON AND PAUL MCCARTNEY

In the past, we tried to solve all our problems by gambling. We wanted our children to have the biggest pool. For our spouse, it may have been a new home or the nicest clothes. Then, we wouldn't have any worries. Nothing but the best for my family, we thought. We would all be one big, loving happy family.

This rationale never worked. Because love can't be bought with things. Loneliness can't be eased by a big win. Families can't be built on money. Instead of happiness, gambling brought us more loneliness than we dreamed.

We didn't win. We lost.

I know material goods can't ease loneliness.
I will work on my relationship with myself
and those I care about.

September 3

Feelings are like babies. They are so sensitive, raw and vulnerable.

LYNN O.

Most of us go through life covering up our feelings. We usually conceal them by playing various roles. Responsible child. Achieving grownup. Happily married spouse.

We've thought that by burying our feelings we would be accepted by others. They would love us because we were the way they wanted us to be.

Now, in recovery, we are allowing our feelings to surface. To be born so that we can discover who we are. Like a baby, we are continuously growing in recovery. Our feelings need to be tended to. We need to nurture ourselves and care for our feelings.

~

I know I am alive and full of feelings.
I will nurture my feelings and allow them to surface.

September 4

"Perhaps the world's second worst crime is boredom;
the first is being a bore."
SIR CECIL BEATON

When we were actively participating in our gambling addiction, we thought life was exciting. We moved in fast circles and were involved in the highs that this type of lifestyle brought.

Recovery doesn't have to mean boredom. Life is still exciting. It's just that the highs aren't as dramatically high as when we were gambling. And the lows aren't as overwhelmingly devastating. Instead, we are living on the even, peaceful wave of serenity.

It is my responsibility to define my recovery. Do I bore my Gambling Anonymous group with the old me and the same old stories. Or do I bring a new and exciting find about life to share with others each week?

~

I know that serenity need not be boring.
I will remember the sadness of the past
and find happiness in my recovery.

September 5

The first problem for all of us, men and women,
is not to learn, but to unlearn.
GLORIA STEINEM

We come into recovery with a strong base of family of origin issues. Some of us came from single parent families, some were raised by guardians, come had both parents in their lives. The number doesn't matter. Because we all share a common base: we were brought up in dysfunctional family systems.

We can't undo our past childhood. That's gone. We can, however, reflect on it, release it and move on. Staying with the beliefs we learned in our family system will keep us stuck. An unhappy. At best, we will only experience partial recovery.

We need to accept the past rules and begin to define and learn new living skills. We need to get in touch with what we believe, think and feel. We must identify goals and emotional needs. We have to learn to experience and live our lives—not repeat someone else's.

~

I will remember that I am not responsible
for the dysfunction of my childhood.
I will release the past and focus on learning about me.
About my life.

September 6

I was given courage, a sense of adventure
and a little bit of humor. I have a wonderful life.

INGRID BERGMAN

Stepping into cool ocean waters, we wait in dreaded anticipation for the cold waves to hit our body. After the initial temperature shock, our body adjusts to the water.

So it is with many of the steps we take in our recovery program. A lot of times, we muster up a good measure of courage in order to take the tiniest step forward. After the initial step, we adjust to the new feelings we generated in our risk taking and continue on life's path.

It doesn't matter what the outcome of our steps are. Because the outcome is out of our control. What matters is that we have the courage to take the necessary steps and then learn from the outcome. For whatever decision we make, there will be an outcome.

~

Today I will have the courage to take a step forward and learn from the outcome.

September 7

And I'm proud to be an American where at least I know I'm free.

LEE GREENWOOD

Freedom means choice. Each day, we make many choices in our lives. What to have for breakfast. Whether to go to work. When to fill the car with gas.

Undeniably the best choice we made was to no longer give in to our gambling addiction. We chose abstinence. We chose recovery. We chose freedom from gambling. We are where we're at today because this is where we chose to be.

~

Today I am thankful for the opportunity
to make my own choices.
I am thankful I chose recovery.

September 8

There's a period of life when we swallow a knowledge of ourselves and it becomes either good or sour inside.

PEARL BAILEY

Step 10 of our recovery program encourages us to continue to take a personal inventory. This self-evaluation is crucial to our growth. By looking at ourselves regularly, we can stay on the path to peace.

Taking a personal inventory doesn't mean pointing out all the bad we've done. Rather, it means reflecting on our decisions. Could we have improved on them? What can we learn from our experiences? How can we make our relationships with others better?

Taking a personal inventory also means pointing out the good. Affirming that we are beautiful human beings who bring much to this world.

~

Today I will spend some time reflecting on my behavior. What am I doing to make my life more serene?

September 9

Life is like a jigsaw puzzle but you don't have the picture on the front of the box to know what it's supposed to look like. Sometimes, you're not even sure if you have all the pieces.

ROGER VON OECH, PH.D.

Jigsaw puzzles come in a variety of sizes. Some have as few as six pieces. Others can have over a thousand. We always know the number of pieces and the outcome of the puzzle by the cover on the box.

Life also has many pieces. They're called days in our lives. We don't know the number of pieces in our life because it's not written on any box cover.

We do know what the picture looks like in recovery, though. By working our program one day at a time, we know the outcome is serenity, fulfillment and happiness.

I don't know how many pieces are in the puzzle of my life. I do know each day in my recovery program creates a picture of serenity today.

September 10

*The erosion of feelings is likened to the erosion of a river bank.
When the soil is gone, it's gone.*

MARY B.

We've been at that place where we're indifferent. Life is coming down around us. We can't feel. Slowly, steadily,, our gambling addiction eroded our feelings.

Like commercial equipment can help rebuild a river bank grain by grain of sand, we, too, can learn in recovery to identify our feelings one by one. We can bring them out and learn about us.

Feelings are our most personal and treasured possessions. We should not suppress them. For bringing them to the surface allows us to feel them and know our true identity. We can own them.

~

I will not suppress what I feel.
I will identify my feelings and allow myself to feel them.
For it is only in feeling that I can experience life.

September 11

Regardless of what you say or do,
some of the people will hate you all the time.

JAMES A. BARR

In our lives, we sought approval from many people—our parents, friends, the boss, our spouse. We were on a course of constantly trying to be pretty enough, witty enough, responsible enough, rich enough, successful enough.

In reality, enough was still never enough. Because when we reached the point where enough should have been, the point was raised. And, the vicious circle started again.

When we seek approval from others, we only stay on the treadmill of pain. When we let go of the need for approval from others, we allow ourselves to experience approval from within.

~

I know that approval comes from inside me.
I approve of me.

September 12

He was never quite at home. But, he gave us many.

LUCILLE BALL

Responsibility takes many forms. Before beginning our journey in recovery, we may have been good at providing things—a home, cars, the newest electronic gadgets.

But what was missing was our responsibility to our relationships with others. Because when we are involved in relationships, we have a responsibility to it and those involved with us. It doesn't mean being accountable for the total relationship. Rather, it means being responsible for our part in it.

I understand that I share responsibility
in the relationships I have with others.
I accept that responsibility.

September 13

There's no way that what people see on celluloid
has anything to do with me.

PAUL NEWMAN

Video cameras are everywhere these days. Recording a baby's first steps. Taking comments from guests at a party. Making a record of our past.

What was in our past was our gambling addiction. There are many things about the record of our past that can't be erased like a video tape, though.

Today, we are adding new pieces to our past. First steps that carry us further into our serenity. Steps that we want to live on.

~

I know I can't erase the past recordings of my life.
But, I can add recovery and serenity to my tape of life.

September 14

Humbly asked God of our understanding to remove our shortcomings.

STEP 7

Why do we need to remove our shortcomings? Because the continual existence of these shortcomings take us one way—back to compulsive gambling. We've used compulsive gambling in the past to attempt to relieve ourselves from our issues. It didn't work then. And it won't work now.

Our Higher Power will help us. We have to do the work. And ask for guidance.

~

I will ask my Higher Power for assistance and guidance.
I will rid myself of my destructive shortcomings.

September 15

We can't face life backward, we have to face life forward.

JOE A.

History isn't found only in the classroom. We each have a history. It's what formed us into who we are today.

In recovery, we don't wipe out our history and go from there. Instead, we look at our background and work with the issues and feelings. Then, we let go of them and work on our growth in serenity and happiness.

Our pre-recovery history won't disappear. We know it was traumatic. But, each day in our recovery program, we are creating happier days to add to our history. Our history now includes peace.

Today I will add a day to my history.
A day of serenity.

September 16

When you tell a story, do you often exaggerate or embellish it?
THE BOOK OF QUESTIONS

At times we've added "a little something extra" to stories we've told. Perhaps we said we won a bigger jackpot that was real. Maybe, we said our luxury car got more miles to the gallon than it really did.

The point is, we needed to be grandiose. To feel important. Puff our chests out. It was as if the truth wasn't good enough. Wasn't acceptable.

We now know the truth is good enough. Telling the truth means we also know we are good enough. That different words and greater stories won't make us better people.

I will tell the truth.
Doing so means I respect myself.

September 17

Everything we do in life is based on fear, especially love.

MEL BROOKS

How many times have we thought if we didn't act the way someone else wanted us to, they wouldn't love us? So, out of fear of not being loved, we acted out or did things against our wishes seeking love and approval.

But true love really isn't based on fear. Love is kind. Love is caring. Love is respect for another's boundaries.

I know that love is freedom.
Fear imprisons me.
True love releases me.

September 18

Nothing that a man does takes him lower
than when he allows himself to fall so far as to hate anyone.

MARTIN LUTHER KING, JR.

Everyone has had wrongs done to them. As a child, someone may have broken our favorite toy. As an adult, someone may have lied about us. Or made a promise to us and then didn't keep it.

We can be angry, yes. But we need to work through our anger and let go of it. Hating others takes up a lot of our energy. And it gives them power over our emotions and feelings. Power over us. Over our lives.

Is that what we want? To give others control?

~

I will work through my anger.
I realize hating another uses up my energy.
I will take my power back.
I will work today not to give my power away.

September 19

Warm cookies and cold milk are good for you.
ROBERT FULGHUM

We all need nurturing. Before our involvement in recovery, we tried to take care of those needs with the highs gambling brought. It was easy to temporarily forget about the lows that were part of the deal, too.

In recovery, we know that we need to take care of ourselves. To nurture the child within us. To look at our needs and feelings. Identify them and work through them.

Nurturing isn't being selfish. In fact, it means being generous. With ourselves. To find out who we really are and allow that person to grow in recovery.

Today I will spend time taking care of me.

September 20

Don't ever eat where they don't want to feed you.

PHIL CARLSON

We all have emotional needs. In the past, we tried to get those needs met through our involvement in compulsive gambling.

We know now that it doesn't have to be that way. Some of our emotional needs are met by us. Others request the support of others around us.

But, some of the people in our lives can't give us emotional support. They may be struggling in their own addiction. It is not our place to judge. Rather, we need to realize that we need to place ourselves in healthy situations and relationships. That may mean making new, healthy friendships.

I know that I must keep myself involved
in healthy relationships. I won't look for
nurturing from those who cannot provide it.

September 21

Good girls like bad boys.

SUE J.

Why do we believe that we deserve to be treated poorly? Most likely, our family of origin gave us these messages. Messages that we weren't good; we'd never amount to anything. Messages that ate away at our self worth.

Is it any wonder, then, that we gravitated toward partners and relationships that were unhealthy? Since that's the best we though we could do, we settled for it.

Today, we know that we are worth more than abusive, demeaning treatment. We are worthy of respect, of love, of goodness and serenity in our lives.

~

My self worth will not rest with messages
given to me in my youth. I am a worthy human being
and deserve the best life has to offer.

September 22

Modesty is a vastly overrated virtue.

JOHN KENNETH GALBRAITH

We have been brought up to believe that it was wrong to praise our accomplishments. Perhaps we were told we shouldn't talk positively about ourselves. We carried these thoughts into adulthood, denying the many good things about us.

This kind of treatment teaches us not to accept ourselves as unique, wonderful individuals with much to offer. But, the real truth is we are just that. Our thoughts count. We are beautiful, caring, unique people.

~

Today I will look myself in the eye in my mirror.
I will say to myself, "I am a beautiful person
with much to offer myself and others. I am acceptable."

September 23

I think most people are more important than their opinions.

JORGE LUIS BORGES

Some people think the way we do. Some do not. That doesn't make them right. It doesn't make us wrong. We're all entitled to our opinions.

If we are patient and look beneath the surface of other's opinions, we may be surprised at what we find. It could be a lonely, scared person, crying out for help.

We should think back to our own behavior and opinions before we sought help from our gambling addiction. What did others find beneath our cover of opinions?

~

Today I will exercise patience and tolerance with others whose opinions are different from mine.
I know I need not to give up my personal boundaries to do so.

September 24

The question of suicide. Keep it a question. It's not really an answer.

MELBA COLGROVE, PH.D.

Many compulsive gamblers are overwhelmed by despair until it seems that the only possible way out is suicide. But, suicide is the end. Of everything. No more chances.

We chose another direction. Recovery. Because recovery is a beginning. A chance for us. The only one we have that guarantees us serenity, peace and a healthy life.

I know recovery is the only answer.
I am thankful I found the answer.

September 25

What a lovely surprise to finally discover
how unlonely being alone can be.

ELLEN BURSTYN

A lot of us never learned to be alone with ourselves. We surrounded ourselves with people and relationships—anything to keep from being alone—and lonely.

But, how many times have we been alone in our relationships with others. Being with someone doesn't guarantee freedom from loneliness.

We need to look to ourselves first for companionship. We need to identify for ourselves who we are; for it is in accepting ourselves for who we are that we are now self-defining. We no longer need others to define who we are.

~

I know being alone with myself doesn't have to be lonely.
I will spend sometime with myself today.

September 26

Only the man who does nothing makes no mistakes.

JERRY LEWIS

Risk taking and reward go hand-in-hand. In our active compulsive gambling days, we risked a lot. We also lost a lot—money, maybe family, but most certainly self-esteem.

Risk taking doesn't have to be a lose-all proposition. And, the risks don't have to be gigantic. Sometimes, we take a little risk and get a little reward. But, it's a reward just the same.

What happens when we risk and things don't turn out the way we wanted? Where do we find our reward?

The answer is in the step forward we took in risking. We moved ahead in our personal recovery program.

~

I know that by taking risks
I am learning and moving forward in my recovery.

September 27

I lost my moral compass.
JEB STUART MAGRUDER

Abstinence from compulsive gambling is key in our personal recovery program. But, there is more. Step 4 says, "made a searching and fearless moral and financial inventory of ourselves."

Before recovery, we compromised our beliefs or morals in hot pursuit of our gambling addiction. For many of us, to the point of losing them completely.

Now, we must clarify for ourselves what our basic beliefs and morals really are. What do we stand for? It is in this process that we begin to develop our identity. Because it is from this identity "self image" from within ourselves that we work a program of recovery. Remember, recovery starts from within and we now have internal reference points for living.

~

I know abstinence is the first piece
of my recovery program. Today, I will also focus
within on my personal beliefs or morals.
To walk what I talk.

September 28

God doesn't make any losers.
TOM LANDRY

Did you ever try to beat yourself up? Maybe you think that your should be farther in your program. Maybe you want a better job. Maybe you condemn yourself for neglecting your family.

But, stop for a minute and think of all the things you've done right for yourself. Perhaps you spent an extra 15 minutes reading to your child. Maybe you're taking a course to get a different job someday. Most importantly, though, you're working on your recovery program.

We need to focus on our self-worth and recognize that there is a lot "right" about us today—and every day.

~

I know that I bring a lot to this world with my presence.
There is much that is good about me.

September 29

Competing pressures tempt one to believe that an issue deferred is a problem avoided; more often it is a crisis invited.

HENRY KISSINGER

Sometimes the ocean can be tricky. A young girl floated out into seemingly gentle waves to enjoy being pushed back to the shore by them. Suddenly, she screams, "Daddy," and her father knows she's in trouble—an undercurrent is pulling her away. He rushes out to save her.

There are times in our recovery program where we seem to be treading along comfortably only to be jolted by complications in our path. It can be strong pull or a small tug, but it frustrates us just the same.

Like the girl's father rescuing her, our personal recovery program is there to help us with our difficulties. Continuing to follow our program during these times can lead us back to our serenity.

Today, I will remember that my
personal recovery program gives me
the tools to deal with the bad days.
I know the good days far outnumber the bad.

September 30

All you need is love.
JOHN LENNON & PAUL MCCARTNEY

When we reach step 6 in our recovery program, we are "entirely ready to have our defects of character removed." This is a big step in our recovery because it allows us to begin to love ourselves as we are. Not what we tried to be while feeding our gambling addiction.

Knowing who we are and accepting who we are—with our assets and liabilities—is all that is important. Before we can truly love others, we need self love. If we can't love within ourselves, we can't spread love outside of ourselves.

~

I love myself.
I am a healthy, beautiful human being.

October 1

When people say: she's got everything,
I've only one answer: I haven't had tomorrow.
ELISABETH TAYLOR

Yesterday's gone. Whatever we did with our yesterday is past.

Were we able to take another step forward in our recovery? Did we stumble just a little? Or were we able to simply stay where we were at?

It doesn't matter today. Because it's another day for us. We lived our yesterday. Another opportunity to live our lives to the fullest. What does it mean for us—today?

Today I will live my life fully,
taking it one day at a time.

October 2

When I tried to fix my spouse, I wrecked myself.

JIM K.

We can't fix anyone else. We can spend a lot of time trying, but it only leads to frustration and anger for us.

Thinking back to our own addictive behavior we know that no one could fix us either. Try as our loved ones might, they could not get us to do what they wanted us to.

We decided our lives needed fixing. We sought help for ourselves. And, we work on our own recovery daily.

~

Today I will remember that I am not able
to control another's life. I can be concerned,
but I am responsible only for my own program.

October 3

A calm sea does not produce a skilled sailor.

SAYING ON A PLAQUE

Even in recovery, we come upon obstacles. It may seem at times that we are constantly handed challenges meant to test our determination to remain free from gambling.

Life is a challenge. What we do with those challenges is important. We can give in to them and destroy our lives. Or we can meet them head on and continue to grow in recovery.

~

I know the waters aren't always smooth in recovery,
but I will meet my challenges head on.

October 4

I've got to admit it's getting better. It's getting better all the time.

JOHN LENNON AND PAUL MCCARTNEY

In this world of instants—food, video replay—we may have a tendency to think we can have an instant recovery from our gambling addiction. Wouldn't that be great?

Maybe not. Because when we take baby steps in our recovery program, we learn as we grow. We make many discoveries along the way. Experiences that help to shape and strengthen our recovery process. Small successes on the road to recovery mean serenity and fulfillment.

~

Today, I will be thankful for the small successes I am making in my life.

October 5

Oh, my friend, it isn't what they take away from you that counts—it's what you do with what you have left.

HUBERT H. HUMPHREY

We can be grateful for the new beginning our personal recovery program is giving us. We know we have suffered major losses through our gambling. Money, sure, but more importantly, the loss of self-esteem and self-acceptance. We could find very few reasons for feeling good.

Recovery and gratitude go hand-in-hand. Recovery gives us the chance to define our values, examine our behavior and set personal goals. We begin working with our fear, anger and resentment.

As we do so, our sense of reality returns. We develop new interests, make new friends. Most of all, we begin to experience happiness.

~

Today I will be grateful for the many discoveries
I have made in my recovery program.
I am thankful for what I have left in my life.

October 6

It's nice to be beautiful, but it's beautiful to be nice.

CHRISTOPHER ATKINS

We are all special. With special talents. Some people can write beautiful music. Some can negotiate a significant contract. Some can perform surgery. Some can build a beautiful house.

Our looks aren't important. Those few extra pounds are not important to a child who appreciates the gentle way we wipe their tears away. A balding head won't prevent us from helping an elderly person mow their grass.

The key is to look inside for beauty. Within ourselves and others.

~

Today, I will focus on what is right about me.
There are many things I can do.
I have much to offer.

October 7

Made a list of all persons we had harmed
and became willing to make amends to all.
STEP 8

Who is the number one person on this list? Ourselves. That's because we have harmed ourselves in every way imaginable—financially, spiritually, emotionally, physically.

Next, we have to look at all others in our current or past life. During our compulsive gambling times, it's pretty certain that we've harmed just about everyone we've encountered. Were we mean? Did we lie? Did we steal? Did we make promises we never kept? These are just a few examples of the way we have harmed others.

The good news is that this step will help us to be free of our past and return our lives to normalcy.

~

I know this step is difficult because I am facing
the harms I've caused. I know my work in this step
will bring me stronger in the peace I am living in recovery.

October 8

I have gone through hell, I tell you, a hell no one, no person, no man, no beast, not even a fire hydrant could endure.

JUDY GARLAND

Life as a compulsive gambler is hell. There is absolutely no compliment we can pay this lifestyle. No positive words we can use to describe it.

Simply put, our lives were out of control. The more we tried to control, the less we could do so. We may have even thought of suicide.

At some point, we decided to take the First Step. "We admitted we were powerless over gambling—that our lives had become unmanageable." Instead of a life of total darkness, we felt we could find a glimmer of light somewhere. That's what led us to recovery. That's what keeps us involved in our personal program.

~

I am thankful that my program has led me to release the darkness of my former life. My days are now filled with the light of my personal recovery.

October 9

I don't know what life would be if our only aim was to banish all the difficulties and pain. I suppose that I could lie on a sofa and eat candies until my heart stopped, but that's not my nature. I don't want it that easy. I want to feel that I'm alive!"

LENA OLIN

Step Two of our Twelve Step recovery program states "Came to believe that a Power greater than ourselves could restore us to a normal way of thinking and living." This step doesn't say our Higher Power is going to remove all the problems in our lives and let us live a fairy tale existence. That's not in our best interest.

We'll still face challenges in our lives. But what Step Two does say is that we can release ourselves from the constant struggle that living a life of gambling brought us. When we ask for guidance from our Higher Power, we learn that life doesn't have to be a struggle. With our Higher Power in control, we can restore our lives to a more serene existence for ourselves.

~

I am thankful for the guidance that my
Higher Power provides in living my life.
I face the challenges with a positive feeling
that will allow me to grow in my recovery.

October 10

Everyone must take chances, challenge yourself, and change.
If you don' have a change, you're not growing.
And if you're not growing, you're not really living.
STEPHANIE KRAMER

Growth means change. The changes in our lives may be subtle. They may be baby steps. And, at times, they mean big leaps.

The important thing is to keep ourselves open to change; participate in changes which are appropriate for us. Change keeps us moving forward. Change keeps us living our lives in the best way possible.

I know that change is good for me. I will think back to the biggest change I made in my life—recovery. And I will remember that recovery is allowing me to live my life to the fullest.

October 11

I went to sleep with gum in my mouth and now
there's gum in my hair . . . .
I could tell it was going to be a terrible,
horrible, no good, very bad day.
ALEXANDER

Some days nothing seems to go right. Yesterday, we had a flat tire on the way to work. Or, maybe the baby threw up on us just as we were on our way out the door and we were late for an appointment.

Days are measured in hours. They are also measured in moments. We need to be remind ourselves that not everything goes our way all the time. As the GAM-ANON "Just for Today" reading states: just for today, I will adjust myself to what is, and not try to adjust everything to my own desires. I will take my "luck" as it comes, and fit myself to it . . . just for today I will have a quiet half hour all by myself, and relax. During this half hour, sometime, I will try to get a better perspective of my life."

~

I will count the blessings in my life.
Things don't always go my way,
but I am comforted in knowing many things do.

October 12

I think that one terrifying thing that has happened now
is that the truth has gone out of style.

KATHERINE HEPBURN

Sometimes the truth can hurt. Although we'd like to take our family on a vacation, we may need to face the fact that the budget won't cover this expense at this time. Certainly, they may be disappointed.

But, it's better to tell the truth. In doing so, we allow them to become part of the solution. Maybe the family can't go to a resort, but we may be able to pack a picnic lunch and go to the park to swim, relax and play. Together, we can explore the alternatives and come up with the best answer possible.

Telling the truth sets us free. It allows us to face issues straight on, no matter how difficult that may be. We know in telling the truth we are doing the best we can given our circumstances. There is no shame in the truth.

I will tell the truth, even though it may seem
easier to avoid doing so. In telling the truth,
I am working my personal program.

October 13

Success means never having to admit you're unhappy.

ROBERT EVANS

People measure success in many forms. A new car. Children attending private schools. The biggest house and swimming pool. The grandest vacation. Earning a large salary. Are these definitions of "success" merely a cover up for unhappiness?

Only we can define success for ourselves. Success may mean a loving relationship with our mate. Success may mean a child's laughter. Success may mean facing up to our compulsive gambling and working our personal recovery program. What will bring us the most happiness?

~

Success for many in our society is measured
in materialistic ways. Within me is the
real measuring stick of success:
am I serene, calm, fulfilled, peaceful?

October 14

If you don't stand for something, you will stand for anything.

GINGER ROGERS

Who am I? What role am I playing? Good friend, perfect mate, obedient child, model employee? Whose rules am I playing by; mine or others'?

We need to define and understand our values or principles. If we don't know what they are, we allow others to define who we are and what we stand for. When we compromise those values and principles we identify as our own, we compromise ourselves and, in time, lose our sense of self. Is that how we want to live our lives?

~

I will identify my values. In doing so, I will know who I am. I will not allow others to define me.

October 15

Whether it's the best of times of the worst of times,
it's the only time you've got.
ART BUCHWALD

Yesterday is gone. Tomorrow doe not yet belong to us. Today is what we have. What will we do with our today?

We certainly will have many responsibilities in the course of our "today." Work, family, social relationships, grass to mow, houses to clean. But, let's not let them overwhelm us. Let's not get caught up in these things at the expense of our serenity.

We need to remember our recovery comes first. That's not selfish. Because without our personal recovery, we cannot deal with the other events in our lives. We won't use recovery as an excuse to neglect our responsibilities. We will use our today to take care of ourselves. Then, our ability to attend to these responsibilities will be assured.

My personal recovery is my first priority.
I will focus on my today.

October 16

The trouble is, if you don't risk anything, you risk even more.
ERICA JONG

Risk taking can be uncomfortable. When we risk, we are moving into unfamiliar territory. Out of our comfort zone. Taking a risk can seem like stepping off a cliff into the unknown.

Not taking risks means staying where we are. Being stuck in a life that is unhealthy for us.

Risk taking means growth. We took a risk in making a decision to enter a recovery program for compulsive gambling. That was a big risk for us. We were not sure what the recovery would bring. Now, we are.

We all begin with little risks. Maybe we can't strike up a conversation with a someone, but we can say hello. As we grow stronger, we will be more comfortable taking bigger risks.

~

Today, I will take a risk. I will smile and say hello to someone.
I will move out of my comfort zone
and ahead in my growth.

October 17

You can't be serious 24 hours a day.
You have to take half an hour or an hour a day to be childish.
VLADIMIR HOROWITZ

Life can be too serious. We face recovery issues and life's challenges every day. And, although things get better in our program, life will always provide many interesting opportunities for us.

Even though we are adults, many of us have never been children. Our innocence and ability to experience life on a children's level were taken from us. Childhood wasn't fun for us. We don't know how to have fun.

We need to give ourselves permission to laugh. To be silly. To have fun. To take off the adult rules we've placed on ourselves and have a good time.

~

Today, I will make time to have fun.
I give myself permission to laugh and enjoy myself.

October 18

I have a tough time expressing anger to people. Sometimes I wish I could raise my voice a little, but I just get quiet or become amusing.

WOODY ALLEN

Throughout our lives, we've learned to suppress our anger in many ways. We were the neighborhood clown, always ready with a practical joke or story. Or, we checked out of the situation, becoming very quiet and introverted. Maybe, we directed it on others not connected with the anger in the first place.

Whatever our method of masking our anger, the thing we did not do is learn to deal with it. Identify our anger. Experience our anger (as in feel it). Release our anger in a healthy way.

We may have learned that it wasn't appropriate to show we were angry. That it was bad. And, if we allowed ourselves our anger, it meant we were bad.

Anger is about feeling our feelings. Anger isn't bad. We aren't bad. Keeping anger inside is destructive to ourselves and our relationships with others.

I recognize that getting angry does not make me
a bad person. I am learning to acknowledge
and feel my feelings in a healthier way,
moving forward in my growth.

October 19

Almost anything is easier to get into than to get out of.

AGNES ALLEN

Compulsion is easy. We know that from first hand experience. Just thinking about our next gambling event could bring us a sudden rush of excitement. We were on top of the world.

Inevitably, we had to come down. The results of our compulsion were that we had done some things we were not too proud of, and would have difficulty repairing the damage. So, we solved the problem with another round of compulsive gambling.

Some of the hardest things in the world to do, however, can truly be the most rewarding. Take our decision to face our compulsion. We work hard in our program. We know the recovery is something we do not have to "get out of." Because by "getting in" and staying in, we can forgo the fleeting thrills of compulsion and discover the stability of serenity.

~

I see compulsion for what it is: a momentary high.
I am happy for the decision I made to work
on a more stable, serene life for myself.

October 20

You have to have the courage to be poor.

BERENICE ABBOTT

Our program brings us many challenges. We are experiencing the comfort of our freedom from compulsive gambling, but we also know that there are "real world" hurdles we must pass.

We have faced our creditors, establishing a payment program to them that will allow us to clear up our debts. But that may leave us feeling that we are doing without all of the material goods and "fun" we used to experience when we were gambling.

We must remember that the material goods and fun were part of the "highs" we felt and they were always, always followed by lows. The progress we make each day keeps us serene. We accept the steady, consistent passage from a life filled with turmoil and pain to a life that allows us to experience happiness and comfort.

~

I accept that I am making steady progress
from my life of desperation. I am experiencing
the satisfaction of settling the issues created
with my gambling. I find contentment in this discovery.

October 21

Nothing has a stronger influence on their children than the unlived lives of their parents.

CARL JUNG

Perhaps our parents had many difficulties growing up. They, through no fault of their own, never had an opportunity to nurture the child within themselves.

People pass on what they know. They may have wanted a life better for their children than themselves, but without knowing what that better life is, they cannot begin to improve things for their children.

The point is not to blame. The point is to look at our role models. This is where we learned our living and coping skills. Through our recovery program, however, we can nurture the child within and improve our own lives.

~

I will remember that my parents did the
best they could with what they
experienced with their parents.
I will not look at them for the things
that went wrong with my life; rather,
I will look to myself to
make things right with my life.

October 22

If you demand perfection from them, you will demand perfection from yourself, and you will be miserable all your life.

LOUISE L. HAY

We don't live in a perfect world. Yet, we want perfection from those around us and from ourselves. Others can't measure up to the standards we place on them. They are our standards, not theirs. And, we will never be able to measure up to perfection, either, because when we think we're "there," we just raise the standards a little higher. And a little more out of reach.

Is perfection what we really want? Or is it happiness? Contentment? Pleasure in the life we live and the people who are important to us?

We need to take the focus off of perfection and put it on reality. We live in the real world, not the "perfect" world, whatever that may be. The real world gives us challenges. It allows u to fail and still hold our head up high. The real world allows us to grow. And to find happiness.

~

Life's treasures are found in a real world
that gives me the opportunity to experience
many things. And, it provides many pleasures.

October 23

Old habits have tremendous pull.

STEPHEN R. COVEY

Compulsive gambling is a game of deception. We deceived others into thinking we were going to pay the electric bill when, in fact, we used the money to place a bet that would bring us even more money. And then, we lost. Both the money and the respect of those who are important to us.

Even worse, we deceived ourselves. We thought we could control our gambling and the luck of winning. We shot for the big win and received an even bigger loss.

Old habits do die hard. Not because we like those habits, but because they are more familiar to us. Growth means taking risks. Recovery means facing ourselves. No more deception. Only honesty.

~

I will take the extra steps necessary to be truthful. Today I will be honest with myself and others.

October 24

Money is like a sixth sense without which
you cannot make a complete use of the other five.

W. SOMERSET MAUGHAM

Our compulsive gambling has caused us many living problems. We were behind in bills. We have borrowed from friends, neighbors, family members and every credit source we can think of. We feel shameful about these activities.

In our recovery process, we have faced this issue. We have worked out a plan of payment to those we owe. It may be that we are taking little steps towards what we think is a large debt. But, we are making those steps steadily and consistently.

In doing so, we don't have to worry each time we hear the phone ring that it is someone we owe money to. We will begin to see that others believe in our word that we are becoming trustworthy. Perhaps for some, for the first time.

~

I may be repaying those I owe on a slower basis,
but I release the shame I may have felt
when the situation seemed hopeless.
I take pride in my commitment
to settle my debts bit by bit.

October 25

My wife seems to want to stay on the treadmill of pain.

RAY B.

Sometimes it seems that the more progress we make in our recovery, the more we recognize the struggle and difficulty that others in our life are having in their own recovery process. It can be frustrating to watch a loved one stay stuck in their own "pain" when we have found serenity and joy in our recovery program.

We can only work on our own recovery process. We can support the efforts of our loved ones in their recovery, but they must make their own choices.

~

I will remember that recovery is an individual choice.
I can hope for the best for my loved ones,
but the decision is theirs.

October 26

Be kind to yourself. Begin to love and approve of yourself.

LOUISE L. HAY

Too often we look for approval from others. Will our parents like what we do? Does the boss think we're good?

Approval comes from within. So does love. When we do the best we can in a situation, we can feel good about ourselves, no matter what the outcome is. We deserve and will be rewarded with the ultimate approval—from ourselves.

~

Love and approval come from within.
I love and approve of myself today.

October 27

Say you're sorry when you hurt somebody.
ROBERT FULGHUM

I'm sorry. Two simple words that are the hardest to tell someone. Because they mean that we are not perfect. We have faults.

We didn't set out to intentionally harm anyone. But, we may have, with our words and actions. We can't take back the hurt we caused. We can let those we hurt know we feel badly about the pain we've caused. Saying "I'm sorry" is a step towards healing the wounds—theirs and ours. Our active participation in our program will show them with action that we mean the words we speak.

~

I may not be able to make an involved apology to those I've hurt, but I will let them know I'm sorry.

October 28

It is not the days in your life, but the life in your days.

ADLAI STEVENSON

I have two cars; the Smiths have three. My brother's house is larger than mine. We can't go on an elaborate vacation like my boss.

While we look at what others have, and we supposedly do not, have, we need to consider a few more things. When was the last time the Smiths spent some family time with their children? How come my brother is seldom at home? Why does my boss rarely smile?

The point is not to judge others, but to be thankful for what we do have. We need to look inside for happiness and not focus on what others in our lives may appear on the surface to have. They, in fact, may be lacking what we have—a life filled with peace and serenity.

~

I will live my life to the fullest,
thankful that I have taken my life back to live.

October 29

Blame is one of the surest ways to stay in a problem.
In blaming another, we give away our power.

LOUISE L. HAY

Sometimes life isn't fair. Our parents may have had their own addiction or co-dependency problems. They couldn't parent us in a healthy, positive way.

We can acknowledge that our upbringing was less than perfect. But, if we live in the shadow of blame, we cannot move into the sunlight of life. We are giving others the power over our lives—power to make us miserable.

We can recognize the trials others have placed in our lives. But, we also need to recognize that others can no longer have control over our lives. In doing so, we put the power where it belongs with ourselves.

~

I take back the power in my life.
In doing so, I release the hold
others may have had on me.

October 30

My idea of exercise is a good brisk sit.

PHYLLIS DILLER

Each of us face a number of stressors every day—my car broke down; a major project at work is due; the baby is ill; I had to face a creditor. In the past, we would stuff our feelings inside. But, at some point they would be released by our compulsive gambling behavior.

Exercise is a good way to help release stress and keep ourselves physically and emotionally well. We don't need to be marathon runners, two hour weight lifters or any other type of super athlete. A good 15 minute walk will get us up, out and moving, plus help release our stress. Even on days we are not stressed, regular exercise of any kind contributes to our overall fitness and well-being.

An added benefit is that we can enjoy the wonders of our universe along the way. Take a minute to watch the children play, or the birds singing. Enjoy the flowers in bloom.

~

I will set aside some time today to get some exercise and to enjoy the earth's many beautiful blessings.

October 31

Fairy Godmother, where were you when I needed you?

CINDERELLA

No one makes our choices for us. We chose to gamble, maybe using the mortgage or food money to place a bet or get to a machine looking for the big win that would take care of all our problems and pull us out of our desperation.

We also chose recovery. And we continue to choose it every day. Sometimes the road to recovery gets a little rough and we struggle to stay on the path. But, we choose to work our program and are rewarded with its many positives.

The choices we make to keep us healthy give us the chance we want for a happy, contented life.

~

I am thankful for the choice I made to seek help.

November 1

You got to be very careful if you don't know where you're going, because you might not get there.

YOGI BERRA

Where am I going? How am I going to get there? What path will this recover process take for me? I have so many questions.

Recovery has the answers to all of our questions. All we have to do is trust, believe and follow our individual program. Instead of trying to control, we must just let go and work our program. We turn ourselves over to our Higher Power. We turn ourselves over to the strength of recovery.

By following our program, we know where we are going. We're on the path of recovery. It leads us daily to a place where we can find relief from the difficulties we've struggled with. We're growing stronger every day.

~

I know where I am going.
Each day in recovery I am going towards a life of joy.

November 2

Never succumb to the temptation of bitterness.

DR. MARTIN LUTHER KING, JR.

With all the anguish we've suffered while involved in our gambling, it is easy to let bitterness set in. After all, our gambling overtook our lives, controlling our every thought and action. We lost money, property and loved ones. How can we not be bitter?

The past is the past. We can't change what was. What we can change, however, is today. We need to look at what is. The changes we make in our "todays"—whether small or large—create our future, our tomorrows. It is a future free of the pain we suffered in our compulsive gambling.

~

Bitterness has no place in my life.
I am making my future
with the changes I'm making today.

November 3

I talk in male; she talks in female.

BILL S.

Perhaps our family of origin conditioned us into masculine or feminine roles. Boys are tough; they don't cry. Girls take care of others; they don't let anyone know things aren't right.

Both of these mean the same thing: we were not allowed to feel. And, consequently, we can't express our feelings. It doesn't really matter if we were male or female.

Getting in touch with our feelings releases us to know who and what we are. Feeling allows us to grow. And to communicate those feelings to others. In universal words.

Today I will acknowledge my feelings
and know that they are an important part of me.

November 4

Dream what you dare to dream.
Go where you want to go.
Be what you want to be.
SAYING ON A PLAQUE

Dreams can take us many places. For some, it may be to a far away destination. To others, it may mean they are famous. To still someone else, it may mean they are happy.

Dreams can come true. In recovery, we may dream that we remain free from the chains of compulsive gambling. And each day that we take a step further in recovery, we ensure our freedom for another day.

When we are wide awake, we can reinforce our recovery, too. Affirmations can keep us growing positively in recovery.

~

I am living my dream of a life
free from compulsive gambling.

November 5

The easiest kind of relationship for me is with ten thousand people. The hardest is with one.

JOAN BAEZ

Intimacy is difficult. We've avoided it in the past by turning our attention to compulsive gambling. After all, if I focus on feeding my addiction, I don't have to focus on a relationship with anyone, including myself. My relationship is compulsive gambling.

In order for me to be successful in my recovery, I need to put the focus on me. I need to develop a relationship with myself. By doing so, I can then acknowledge my success. Each step I take in recovery will be rewarded internally with the knowledge that I am worth loving. Having an intimate relationship with me will allow me to eventually participate in intimate relationships with others. That will come later. Right now, I am the person I need to develop an intimate relationship with.

~

I commit today to get to know myself better.
I want a relationship with myself.

November 6

Continued to take personal inventory
and when we were wrong, promptly admitted it.

STEP 10

Each day we need to look at ourselves. Not once a month. Or once a week. Every single day.

This allows us to maintain our serenity. Every day. It doesn't mean we are trying to be perfect. After all, perfection isn't the answer.

Growth is. And we grow in our recovery program by being willing to admit our wrongs and correct them.

~

I will take an inventory today. I will admit my mistakes and grow by correcting them.

November 7

You grow up the day you have your first real laugh at yourself.
ETHEL BARRYMORE

Recovery is serious business. Each day we are putting our attention on keeping ourselves free from compulsive gambling. That means distancing ourselves from the behaviors that will lead us back into our habit. We need to stay completely away from that place, where everything about it shouts for us to gamble. We need to stop meeting up with that person that encourages us to "play just this once." For we know that once leads to twice, to three times, to too many times.

What about fun? Did we give that up, too, when we committed to recovery? Absolutely not. In fact, it is important for us to have some fun. To laugh. We just need to understand what fun is—and isn't. After all, were we really having fun in our compulsive gambling? Or, were we distracting ourselves so we wouldn't know we weren't having fun?

~

I will redefine my idea of fun. I will make sure I include real fun in my life.

November 8

When the sun comes up, I have morals again.

ELAYNE BOOSLER

Each of us has a compulsive gambling trigger. Or two. Or many. Sometimes we gambled because it was dark. Or because we were with friends who encouraged us to gamble. Maybe we gambled because we got a promotion at work and we were feeling happy. Any excuse would work for us when we wanted to gamble.

Then, our behavior changed. Things we would never consider doing became quite ordinary while we were gambling. Our morals gave way to our addiction. Gambling led us on a path we didn't want to be on, yet we couldn't figure out how to get off of.

In recovery, we've stepped off the gambling path and onto a new one. The path we're on now leads us to a life of serenity. Each and every day.

~

I am walking the path of recovery.
Each and every day and night.

November 9

I don't want life to imitate art. I want life to be art.

CARRIE FISHER

While gambling, our addiction dictated our life. Everything we did centered around gambling. Responsibilities, including jobs, bills and relationships took a back seat to gambling. It was the most important thing in our life. It was the only thing. It was our life.

No more. We chose to be an active participant in our life. We made the decision to work our recovery program. Although we surrendered control of our life to our Higher Power, we made the choice to take recovery over addiction. It's a decision that offers us hope. It's the right choice. It's the only choice.

~

I want to live my life. I refuse to let gambling dictate my life. I chose to let recovery dictate my life.

November 10

The worst part of success is to try
to find someone who is happy for you.
BETTE MIDLER

Recovery changes us. Isn't that what we want? Isn't that exactly what we begged for when we surrendered to our Higher Power?

It certainly is. Yet, as we get stronger and clearer, we think the people around us are changing. Are they really? Or is it that we are changing and they are staying the same?

Many people in our life will challenge our recovery. They may not have liked the person we were in our addiction, but that was the person they knew and were comfortable with, even though it was uncomfortable. This new person we are is someone they are unfamiliar with. They may try to sabotage our recovery, thinking they can return us to our old self.

Our goal is not to judge them. It is, however, to remain centered on our recovery. That means removing those obstacles that prevent us from working our program. That means distancing ourselves from those people who don't want us to succeed.

~

I am succeeding in my recovery. I will surround myself with others who support me in recovery.

November 11

No matter how big or soft or warm your bed is,
you still have to get out of it.
GRACE SLICK

Life can sometimes be overwhelming. We're working all the overtime we possibly can to catch up, but it seems we are always behind where money is concerned. Or, the kids are sick, causing us to miss a day of work and lose that precious pay. It takes every ounce of our patience to deal with our children and work our program.

The main thing is not to give up. Each step we take—no matter how small—is a step forward in recovery. Each payment we make is one less dollar we owe. Each day the kids are healthy is one more day we are able to work. We have to recognize the positives in our life and celebrate them.

We have a choice. We can choose to buckle under to the obstacles that are in our path. Or, we can work through them—even a little bit—moving us forward in our recovery.

~

I am out of my bed. I am facing the obstacles I may come upon today and celebrating the good in my life.

November 12

Instant gratification is not soon enough.

MERYL STREEP

I want it now. I want that car, that house, that job, that partner, that boat, that swimming pool. On and on it goes. Instead of looking at what we do have, we set our sights on what we think we want. What we think we are lacking. We're constantly trying to live in the future.

That's "if only" thinking. Things would be better "if only" I get that job. "If only" I can buy that house. "If only I can come back."

How are we ever going to get to the future if we aren't present in today? Do I own a house? Maybe not. But, do I have a place to sleep? Certainly. Do I have a brand new car? No, but I have a darn good used car. Maybe it has a little rust, but the motor works and the tires are good. This car will get me where I need to go. Do I have a lot of money? No, I'm not wealthy. Am I released from my compulsive gambling today? Yes! That is my today.

~

I am happy for what I have today. I will take time to enjoy and be thankful for my today.

November 13

Why is it when we talk to God we're said to be praying, but when God talks to us we're schizophrenic?

LILY TOMLIN

Our Higher Power plays a key role in our recovery. To begin our recovery process, we turn ourselves over to our definition of a Higher Power. Consulting with our Higher Power keeps us on our path. We continually seek assistance. We know we can't do it alone. We tried that and were miserably existing in our compulsive gambling.

That "inner voice" we hear is our Higher Power guiding us in recovery. Letting us know he/she is always present with us. Our Higher Power celebrates our accomplishments with us and won't desert us when we are struggling. When we say our Higher Power is with us every step of the way we know it is truly every single step.

~

I am one with my Higher Power.
I have comfort know my Higher Power will guide me.

November 14

I'm afraid. About getting in touch with me.

CAROLYN J.

As we work through our recovery process, we face ourselves in many ways for the first time. Who will be there? What will we discover?

Without compulsive gambling to mask our feelings, we must face them head on. We must actually allow ourselves to feel our feelings. Own them. And work through them.

As we do so, we continue to discover the wonder of our being. We are truly unique gifts to this earth and those around us. We have much to offer. And, above all, we are healthy.

Although I sometimes get afraid of who I am facing,
I am excited at the opportunity to know me.

November 15

No person is your friend who demands your silence,
or denies your right to grow.
ALICE WALKER

As we begin our journey in recovery, we find we have the support of those who are near to us and want us to give up our compulsive gambling. However, they may not all be clear about what recovery means. They may think it simply means we stop gambling and life for everyone will be wonderful.

We know, of course, it means so much more. It involves us making our personal choices and changes to ensure our success. Some of those choices and changes may surprise others, causing them to react negatively to our recovery. They may even try to sabotage it, thinking they can return us to the person they think they knew and want us to be.

Our goal is to acknowledge their discomfort, recognizing that it is their discomfort, not ours to own. We need to remain firm in our recovery. We can do this best by remaining free of judgment of others and keeping our focus on our recovery process.

I will remain true to my recovery.
It is there I find the peace and clarity I need.

November 16

I was born with music within me.

RAY CHARLES

We've buried much of ourselves in the challenges of compulsive gambling. We thought if we could win the big one, our problems would go away. We continued to try after every loss, knowing we would come back somehow and everything would be all right.

We, of course, found out that gambling doesn't cover up our problems or pain. Gambling may have masked the pain for a short time, but it always resurfaced, usually stronger and deeper. No amount of gambling helped. In fact, it intensified our pain and shame.

Recovery helps us deal with everything. The journey leads us through the pain, shame, hurt and other feelings. We face them head on, working the problems out and feeling the pain. In doing this, we can begin to heal what has haunted us for so long.

~

I will work my program to uncover
what I have buried for so long.
I will feel my feelings and rejoice
in my ability to do so.

November 17

People used to throw rocks at me because of my clothes.
Now they wanna know where I buy them.
CYNDI LAUPER

We will always find people who can find something wrong with us. We've been told by those we hold dear that we aren't ambitious enough, pretty enough, we dress terribly, we're too fat, thin, tall short. The list could easily go on and on.

Remember: our Higher Power created us. Each of us is a unique individual. Full of life and potential. We've just been tuned in to those people in our lives who told us what we should be and do. Who have tried to drag us down and make us feel worthless.

Recovery tunes us into ourselves. We no longer allow others to define us. As we work our program we come to accept ourselves and build on the uniqueness we entered this earth with. We know we are wonderful individuals and that our feelings are valid. We have a right—and responsibility—to feel our feelings. And, to live our life.

Today, I will look to myself and rediscover my uniqueness. I am thankful for me.

November 18

Find out who you are and what you stand for, and learn the difference between right and wrong; be able to weight things.

PRINCE

Coming into recovery, we really don't know who we are. We haven't had to know because every time who we are started to surface, we would bury it with gambling. For a short while, we have been able to hide from ourself. When the gambling stopped, though, we were still there, facing ourself.

Now we are experiencing who we are. It's sometimes scary, a lot of times painful, but we keep going. We move on because we know it is crucial to our success in recovery. We know we have the support of others who are working their program or are otherwise interested in helping us succeed. We know we have to do the work, but they are by our side all the way.

Finally, we are making decisions that are good for us. We know what we stand for. We stand for recovery.

~

I am learning who I am.
I know the first thing I stand for is my recovery.
Everything else will fall into place.

November 19

The race is not always to the swift. . . but to those who keep on running.

SAYING ON A PLAQUE

Some days we just feel like giving up. We work our program daily. When, then are we going to be finished recovering?

The fact is, our personal recovery process is lifelong. Each and every day we work our program means another day that we not only remain clean, but also stronger in our growth.

Peace and serenity are ours. But, we must participate actively in our recovery each and every day. In what way will I participate today?

~

I know it is important to be involved
in my personal recovery every day.
I will keep working today.

November 20

I do my best work when I'm in pain and turmoil.

STING

Pain and turmoil were familiar friends to us during our active gambling days. We were uncomfortable with them, yet they were well-known to us. After all, they were part of us, just like our arm or leg. We knew we didn't like it, but we continued to create it.

We know now that pain and turmoil don't have to be a major part of our life. Through our personal commitment to recovery we work through the forest of pain and turmoil, emerging to discover a life of joy. We understand that serenity is the true way of life for us and rejoice in the peace it brings us. We know we do our best work when we are living a life filled with serenity.

~

I am freeing myself of pain in my life.
I seek a life of serenity today.

November 21

Do you know what my favorite part of the game is?
The opportunity to play."
MIKE SINGLETARY

How many opportunities have passed us by? Did we even see them? When we were gambling, usually not. We were blinded by our attention to gambling. After all, it consumed our life, leaving no time for anything else. The only opportunities we were seeking were those that would allow us to gamble.

Yet, we did recognize the biggest and most important opportunity of our life. The opportunity to find a life of peace and happiness. Some of us came willingly because we knew there had to be something better than the despair we were living in gambling. Others of us were forced into recovery by loved ones or legal authorities when our gambling behavior caught up with us.

It doesn't matter how we got here. What does matter is that we are here working on our recovery. We took advantage of the opportunity to change our life for the better. We didn't let this significant opportunity slip away.

~

I am happy for the opportunities I am offered
in recovery. I willingly accept them.

November 22

A team should never practice on a field that is not lined.
Your players have to become aware of the field's boundaries.
JOHN MADDEN

Boundaries are new and unfamiliar to us. Gambling didn't require us to have any boundaries. We could do, say and think any way we wanted to. And, we did. With no thought to the consequences of our actions. We just moved farther and farther out into the valley of deceit, lies, theft. Whatever it took to support our gambling was our method of operation.

The problem was a boundary-less way of life didn't work for us. It didn't make us happy. It didn't make life simpler or easier. The shame was still there. So were our problems.

In recovery, we are working to recognize boundaries and act appropriately. We are also learning to set boundaries for ourselves. By establishing boundaries and working our program within them, we can be sure we live our life within the parameters of successful recovery.

~

Boundaries are new to me. I am working
to live my life within the boundaries of recovery.

November 23

I wonder if other dogs think poodles
are members of a weird religious cult.

RITA RUDNER

We make a lot of changes in our life in recovery to ensure we can be victorious in our struggle against our gambling addiction. One of those changes is removing people from our lives who want us to continue gambling. To them, we now look like someone they don't know. They can't understand the changes because they are gambling and we aren't

Recovery requires us to eliminate anything from our life that would keep us stuck in gambling. Including people. That's tough. No one will tell us it is easy. We're trying not to judge others because they don't know what we do. They haven't experienced recovery as the only hope for serenity. In working our program, we look and act strangely to them, but it is exactly the "strangeness" we need to ensure our recovery. We have to set our boundaries and stick to them.

~

I will not judge others for what they don't know.
I will find peace in what I know in recovery.

November 24

We must open the doors of opportunity.
But we must also equip our people to walk through those doors.
LYNDON B. JOHNSON

Recovery provides us the opportunity to remove the pain from our life. It also gives us the support we need to work our program and remain free from compulsive gambling.

Recovery is our life. Everything we do revolves around our recovery program. That's because we know recovery works for us. Each feeling we work through, each step we take in recovery keeps us walking the path of hope and peace in our life.

Our program provides us with the equipment we need to work our program. There are opportunities to be with others in their recovery program and support each other. There are materials for us to use. This book is an example of that. The important thing for us to do is recognize the equipment we have available to us and use it to ensure our recovery.

~

Recovery is my opportunity.
I will use the equipment
available to me to life a better life.

November 25

You must do the thing you think you cannot do.
ELEANOR ROOSEVELT

Sometimes it just seems like too much." wailed Judy, "When am I going to be done? When will I be cured?

There is no magic potion for us to take to cure our addiction to gambling. Our addiction was work. We worked constantly to stay ahead of the bill collectors. We worked to tell lies to our loved ones because we missed following through on yet another promise we made to them. We worked to make sure we found money and time to gamble. For what? We lost so much.

Recovery is work, too. We work to feel those feelings we've stuffed inside for so long. Maybe they've been there our whole life. We work to rebuild those relationships our gambling destroyed. We work to rebuild trust in ourself and others. Our work in recovery, though, is well worth the effort.

~

Today I will work my program.
I know that my work in recovery
is worth all the effort I put into it.

November 26

It's kind of fun to do the impossible.

WALT DISNEY

Entering recovery, we thought a life free of the pain we felt was impossible. We were just as sure that staying active in our gambling was impossible. In fact, our whole life seemed impossible.

Walking the path of recovery step by precious step shows us that we made the right choice. Each time we make progress we show ourself that serenity is possible. It is up to us to stay on the path of recovery, working our program a day at a time, an hour at a time, a minute at a time. Whatever it takes. Then the impossible becomes very possible.

~

I am doing the impossible.
Because, I know serenity is possible.

November 27

There is more stupidity than hydrogen in the universe, and it has a longer shelf life.

FRANK ZAPPA

How easy it is to judge others. Why does that guy wear multiple rings in his eyebrow? How could two same gender people become loving partners? Why does she listen to that heavy metal music?

The fact of the matter is, it isn't always me. For all I know, that guy wearing multiple earrings may be the only person who visits the nursing home twice a week to volunteer his time entertaining the elderly. That young girl listening to heavy metal music may be going to school full time and holding down a full time job to help her single mother pay the rent. That same gender couple may check on in their physically challenged next door neighbor every day to make sure everything is o.k.

Our job is not to judge others, but to value the differences in each person who comes into our life in any way. In recovery, we allow others to live their life without our interference as we work our own recovery program.

~

I will think positively of others today,
knowing that their lives belong to them.
I know only the facts of my life.

November 28

The difference between fiction and reality? Fiction has to make sense.

TOM CLANCY

I don't get it", Chelsey said, "it looks o.k. to play outside. It stopped raining. Why do I have to stay inside?" "Well," her mom answered, "the cold temperature has frozen the rain. It is dangerous to be outside. You could easily slip and hurt yourself."

While we were gambling, our reality was fuzzy, too. Deep down we knew we were making poor decisions, yet we could always reason away the warnings our conscious gave us. We could easily justify spending our last five dollars on lottery tickets when we knew we really needed to use it to buy a box of cereal for our kids. We knew the rent needed to be paid, but we figured if we could just hit the big one, we have enough money for a year's rent.

Now, we face life with reality. We are making decisions that people working their program make. We actively listen to our conscience to guide us with our decisions. Doing so keeps us on our path of recovery, free from compulsive gambling. Reality may not always make sense to us, but working our program does. It helps us through all areas of our life.

~

My program is my reality. It frees me
from the clutches of compulsive gambling.

November 29

You can complain because roses have thorns,
or you can rejoice because thorns have roses.
ZIGGY

Many things are going right in our life right now. Can we recognize them? Or, are we caught up in looking at our world in only a negative way? When we look at our job do we think only of the things we don't like about it? Or, do we look at the things we do enjoy and figure that everyone has parts to their job that they don't particularly enjoy?

Our life is about our attitude. We have many choices in how we live. Do we look at people and things through our negativity glasses? That's a choice. Do we look at life positively? That's a choice, too. Either choice is ours to make. The choice we make has a huge impact on how our day will play out.

It doesn't mean we have to look at life through rose colored glasses. We do have to make a decision each and every day about our attitude towards our day. We can face our reality with a bright outlook or a dark outlook.

~

Today, I will look at my attitude. I will adjust it, if necessary, to give myself a positive day.

November 30

"In this age, which believes that there is a short cut to everything, the greatest lesson to be learned is that the most difficult way is, in the long run, the easiest."

HENRY MILLER

I know I have group three times a week right now, but I feel better than I did a month ago. And, I haven't gambled," reasons Angela to herself. "I think I'll just go to group once a week from now on. That should be enough. After all, I have other things to do."

Life is full of short cuts. Our program is not. Each step we take in working our program is important. Each half step we take is important. Each conversation and group we participate in is important. Each reading we do is important. And, each time we pick ourselves up after a small slip and return to working our program is important. Because working all the pieces of our program guarantees our success in finding—and living—a life of peace and serenity. Each of us can look at our program and find shortcuts we think we could make. But, are we willing to risk losing that serenity because we were unwilling to take the longer path? Taking shortcuts makes our program harder, not easier. The easy way is to take each of those steps in peace.

~

I look forward to taking the easy way in my program. I know the easy way is to take each and every step in my program.

December 1

"As I have said, the first thing is to be honest with yourself. You can never have an impact on society if you have not changed yourself. . . ."

NELSON MANDELLA

While actively gambling, it was easy to lie to ourselves. We wanted to believe what we said because we could justify anything if it meant we could gamble. We couldn't understand how others could question our honesty when we had been easily able to fool ourselves into believing we were being truthful. We felt we were being honest because that is what we wanted to believe. It was the only way we could make our life tolerable. For even a minute.

We knew the truth, though. Each time we made up an excuse, each time we told a lie, we knew we were being dishonest. Not only with others. But, also, with ourselves.

In recovery, we face our life with honesty. Lies didn't work for us. Truth, we know will. It isn't always comfortable facing our recovery work honestly. But, it is the only way we can be sure we will know a life of joy, free from gambling. Each truthful step we take in our program makes us more solidly anchored in our recovery. And, that's the honest truth.

~

I lead my life with honesty. I will tell the truth and face the responsibilities of this decision.

December 2

I developed a new philosophy . . . I only dread one day at a time.
CHARLIE BROWN

When we look at a lifetime without gambling in our life, it can look impossible. How will we ever be able to keep ourselves from gambling for 30, 40, 50 years? We think we'll never be able to make it happen.

We don't have to. What we do have to do is stop gambling for one day. Today. Or, for one hour. This hour. Or, for this five minutes. If all we feel we can manage is to stop gambling for this one minute, then we stop for this one minute. We congratulate ourselves and then stop gambling for the next minute. Minute by minute we stop gambling for five minutes, for one hour, for one day. Those days become weeks. Four weeks become one month that we have been free from gambling. Twelve months show us that we have successfully kept ourselves from gambling for one year.

Working our program, we know that each minute is a step forward for us. We may stumble along the way, but if we commit to recovery, we pick ourselves up and keep moving in the direction we started. We don't worry about 20 years from now. We positively work on our today.

~

I am in recovery today. I will work my program today, knowing that it will lead me to recovery tomorrow.

December 3

Sought through prayer and meditation
to improve our conscious contact
with God as we understood Him,
praying only for knowledge of His will for us
and the power to carry that out.

STEP 11

During our active compulsive gambling days, spirituality was non-existent. We were so totally wrapped up in gambling, we couldn't attend to our relationship with our Higher Power.

Through our work in our personal recovery program, we are able to establish and maintain our relationship with God as we know Him to be. Prayer and meditation are key to ensuring communication with our Higher Power.

We know we only have to ask our Higher Power for direction. Listening to our Higher Power will help us in working our recovery program in the best way possible.

I will ask my Higher Power for guidance
in my personal recovery program.
I will follow my Higher Power's
counsel for a life of peace.

December 4

Fear is that little darkroom where negatives are developed.

MICHAEL PRITCHARD

Fear of the unknown can be powerful. Entering recovery, we did not know what we would find. We knew that gambling was creating an impossible life for us. But, we knew that life. We were familiar with the chaos gambling created for us. We were constantly trying to stay ahead of our problems by gambling. It prevented us from having to face our problems for a short period of time. When we stopped, though, they jumped right back in our face.

The treasures recovery brings were unknown to us. We knew we had work to do. We knew we had to face ourselves. We'd done so much damage to our life and to others while gambling.

As we work our program, though, we find that person we never knew—us. We name the fears we have. We face the feelings we have always kept hidden. We work through the pain we've stuffed deep inside for so long. And, we find that we have nothing to fear. We discover that underneath all that pain is a wonderful person who has not been allowed to be who they are, a person willing and excited about facing a world free of the pain gambling has caused.

I will face my fears knowing that working
my program will bring me relief from them.

December 5

The triple is the most exciting play in baseball . . . . Home runs win a lot of games, but I never understood why fans are so obsessed with them.

HANK AARON

Actively gambling, we were always after the big win. It didn't matter what type of gambling we were involved in. The small wins were nice, but the big win would really make a difference in our life. So we thought.

In reality, the reach for the big win kept us losing money we couldn't afford to lose. It made us ignore relationships with our family and friends that should have been important to us. It made us slack off on our responsibilities. Funny thing, too, was that we never made that big win. Or, if we were lucky enough to do so, it didn't make our life better. We were still involved in gambling.

We know now that a life of tranquility is a series of steps. We are always working our recovery program, knowing that it keeps us free from gambling. We know that getting to first base requires moving forward a step at a time. Today maybe we are only able to take one step. That one step is just as worthy in our progress as if we were to get to home plate. One step is a victory for us today.

I will look at my progress in recovery one step at a time.
Each step is important to my serenity.

December 6

These are my new shoes. They're good shoes.
They won't make you rich like me, they won't make you rebound like me,
they definitely won't make you handsome like me.
They'll only make you have shoes like me. That's it.

CHARLES BARKLEY

Sometimes we wish for a life that isn't ours. We figure if we were as rich as others we wouldn't have a care in the world. Everything would be just perfect for us. So, we try to make ourselves as much like others as possible. But, it doesn't make our life better.

That's because we are who we are. We have the life we've created for ourselves. Others have problems just like we do. They may handle them differently than we handle ours. We don't know.

Concentrating on our own life is the best way to bring ourselves a more rewarding life. What are my issues? How can I move forward in my recovery? Not by lusting after the life of another, certainly. By focusing on ourselves and working our own program, we can ensure ourselves the life we want to lead. We can be honest with ourselves and know our life is the best we can possibly live. And know that it is great to be who we are.

I will focus my attention on my life,
working my program. Living my recovery.

December 7

Shoot for the moon. Even if you miss it you will land among the stars.

LES BROWN

"I don't think I can do this. It is so much work. I can't concentrate. I'm crying all the time," complained Jesse. "Is this what recovery is all about?"

Recovery is about feeling our emotions. It is about confronting our demons. The demons that forced us into compulsive gambling. Touching our feelings can make us feel raw, out in the open, unprotected. After all, we've mastered the ability to bury those feelings deep inside ourselves our entire life. Letting them surface is scary. This is unfamiliar to us.

It is significant to our recovery to work through our emotions. Experiencing the feelings we've covered up by gambling allows us to find that place of joy we've been looking for. Each time we go through another feeling we lighten the load we've been carrying. We're able to face ourselves and others knowing that we are allowed to be who we are. To feel what we feel. To live a life free from the suffering being imprisoned in gambling caused.

~

I will work through my feelings, allowing myself
to experience each and every one. I am breaking free
from the shackles of compulsive gambling.

December 8

I don't know the key to success,
but the key to failure is trying to please everybody.

BILL COSBY

We all know the saying, "you can't please everyone." Never is it more true than in recovery. Although we have many in our lives who are pleased we have committed to a life free of compulsive gambling, they may have specific ways in which they want us to live. Their ideas of a gambling-free life may not be a life of recovery. It may be as dysfunctional as our life was while we were gambling.

Our concentration needs to be on our recovery program. Applying ourselves to our program is foremost in our life. The first person we have to please is ourselves and recovery provides us the only opportunity to accomplish this. Surrounding ourselves with people who want us to triumph in recovery is critical. It is also possible. Those who are really interested in supporting our recovery won't make impossible demands on us. They will, however, insist that we do everything we need to in order to remain free of compulsive gambling. By pleasing ourselves through recovery we gain the confidence to live a life with peace of mind.

~

I will please myself by working my recovery program.
I know it is a positive step in my recovery.

December 9

You cannot discover new oceans
unless you have the courage to lose sight of the shore.
SAYING ON A PLAQUE

Old behaviors are destructive for us. They are the very thing that led us into compulsive gambling and kept us there.

Those behaviors, though they cause pain and turmoil in our lives, are familiar to us. We've lived them for so long, they come naturally to us. We don't like them, but we don't know how to rid ourselves of them.

We have to use our courage to take steps away from the old, familiar behaviors and towards the new, unfamiliar behaviors. One step, baby step, at a time. For as we move forward inch by inch in recovery, the new behaviors will become comfortable to us. Pleasantly and naturally so.

~

I know that by removing old, destructive behaviors from life,
I will grow stronger. I have the courage to practice new,
healthy behaviors in recovery.

December 10

It's not your blue blood, your pedigree or your college degree.
It's what you do with your life that counts.

MILLARD FULLER

We came to recovery from all walks of life. Some of us were poorly educated and working for minimal wages. Others completed high school. It could be that we even completed college, perhaps even hold a MBA and successfully make lots of money in our career. Still, we all gambled. Our background didn't matter. Our real life revolved around our compulsive gambling habit.

Now, recovery is our life. It is the most important thing we will ever do in our life. All the education in the world doesn't mean a thing if we aren't working our recovery program. Making the biggest salary we've ever thought possible is meaningless if we continue to gamble. Working our program ensures us we are making progress daily in living the life we truly wanted. Recovery guarantees us a life of serenity. A life without chaos. A life without lies. Recovery means integrity in our lives.

~

I am in recovery because I wanted a life free of chaos.
I am working my program to ensure that goal.

December 11

You miss 100 percent of the shots you never take.
WAYNE GRETZKY

"I was doing so well. I hadn't gambled in months," Dave said. "Then, I joined the senior citizens on a trip to the casino. I told myself I was only going for the company and the buffet. But, I ended up gambling again. I'm so ashamed of myself."

Many of us have slipped. Some are small slips. Some are big slips. The size doesn't matter. We veered off the path our recovery had us on and into the murky mud of gambling. When we did, it brought back all of the old junk we'd been carrying around for so long. We felt worthless, shameful. We felt like a failure.

That's not the truth, of course. Yes, we slipped. We won't make excuses for that. But, we faced our slip and jumped right back on that path of recovery. We recommitted ourselves to our program, knowing it is the only place we can truly be free from compulsive gambling. We took another shot at working our program, another shot at peace. For that we can be grateful.

~

I will acknowledge my missteps.
But, I will also acknowledge my recommitment
to working my program.

December 12

Hem your blessings with thankfulness so they don't unravel.
SOURCE UNKNOWN

What's going right in our world today? Is it cold and rainy outside? We can be thankful we're inside and wearing warm clothing to shield us from the cold. Kids driving us nuts with their loud playing? We can count our blessing that they are healthy and able to happily play together. Did we overcook the hamburgers for lunch? We can be pleased we have food to put on the table and the humor to make it through our overdone burgers.

As rough as it may seem at times in recovery, we still have much to be thankful for. We committed our life over to our Higher Power to free us from compulsive gambling. In doing so, we opened our life to the pleasures around us. They have been given to us in many ways. Each step we take in recovery is a step away from gambling. It is a step towards serenity. It is a step of victory for us.

Throughout the day, we need to take a moment to think about what is going right in our life at that very minute. Maybe not everything we think we like to have going right. But, a lot will be right about our life. We only have to recognize it.

I will look for the things that are right in my life today. I am thankful for all that recovery has brought me.

December 13

Courage is being afraid but going on anyhow.
DAN RATHER

There is so much that is unknown to us when we enter recovery. We know that gambling isn't working for us. How do we know that recovery will? So much has gone wrong in our life. We thought gambling was the answer. We thought that if we could come back from our losses, we could set our life right.

We know recovery will work for us because we admitted we could not do it by ourselves. We surrendered our will and turned our life over to our Higher Power. We don't always know the steps we will take in recovery, but we take comfort in knowing our Higher Power does know. By listening to our Higher Power we are assured that we will walk the path of recovery. Walking that path means having the courage to take each step without asking why. Just believing that our Higher Power has our best interests in mind. Understanding that serenity is ours if we just have the courage to work our program.

~

I will take a courageous step in recovery today.
I will listen to the guidance of my Higher Power.

December 14

Tension is who you think you should be. Relaxation is who you are.
CHINESE PROVERB

Television ads tell us we need to be more wealthy, encouraging us to invest our money with a particular brokerage firm. Cosmetic companies push us to be sexier by wearing their make up or perfume. Automobile firms tell us to be successful we need to drive their brand. Gambling publicity invites us to join them so we can win the big one. On and on it goes. We're surrounded by a world of advice on how much better our life could be if only we would follow them. No wonder there is so much stress in our life! It takes a lot of energy to listen to all these competitors vying for our life.

We need to accept who we are. Working our program teaches us this. We dig deep into our emotions and free ourselves from the pain we've experienced throughout our life. The pain that led us to seek relief by compulsive gambling.

Working our program we discover that who we are is all right. In fact, we're better than all right. We're fantastic. We take that discovery and work with our Higher Power to create a life of peace for ourselves.

I am thankful for the opportunity to create a life for myself that is free from the torture I experienced while gambling.

December 15

Life is really simple, but we insist on making it complicated.
CONFUCIUS

We have an amazing ability to make life much more difficult than it needs to be. We struggle with the need to control every aspect of our daily life. Sometimes we put ourselves on such a precise time scale, that we deliberately set ourselves up to fail. Who can keep up with a grinding schedule of activity after activity? Piling appointments and lessons and meetings on top of an already busy work schedule will send us into an irritable frenzy, lashing out at everyone and everything that gets in our way. It can send us out of control and straight back to our gambling addiction.

We need to look at our life and our recovery. Our program teaches us to simplify our life. First and foremost is our recovery. Which of our daily activities supports that? Are we pushing aside parts of our recovery so we can fit in more non-recovery activities? By using our program as a measure, we can quickly determine those demands on our time that we can eliminate from our life. The result is we lead a more simplified and manageable life. We lead a life of recovery.

~

I will look at my life to see what activities
are necessary to support me in my recovery.

December 16

If I had my life to live over, I would perhaps have more actual troubles but I'd have fewer imaginary ones.

DON HEROLD

During our active gambling, we were excellent at creating problems for ourselves. The rent couldn't be paid because we gambled. Food couldn't be put on the table because we gambled. Commitments couldn't be honored because we gambled. Our life was a mess because we gambled.

We changed all that the minute we entered our recovery program. We'd already proven that gambling wasn't giving us the life we wanted. Recovery shows us how to get our life back in control. If we work our program we learn that our recovery behavior helps us remove the problems and chaos from our life. We don't create problems for ourselves because we are responsible for our actions. For the first time in our life we have the opportunity to jump off that roller coaster of chaos.

~

I will work my program today.
I know it is a smoother path for me.

December 17

What people say, they will have to say it.
I can't do anything about their opinions.
DALE EARNHART

From a very early age, we've been told who we are. We didn't had the chance or support to develop in a family that could give us a solid foundation from which we could grow into healthy children and adults. We may have had a two parent household with a solid roof over our head and food on the table. But, we were starved emotionally. That sent us straight towards an addiction that could medicate our pain, gambling. But, gambling didn't feed our emotional needs. Each time we stopped, we were faced with a sense of loss and shame. So, some of us just stopped growing emotionally all together.

Recovery helps us release the emotional baggage we've grown up with. We learn to peel back the labels others put on us to uncover who we really are. What comes out from under those restrictions is a person able to define who they are with the help of their Higher Power. The definitions others gave us become unstuck, clearing the way for the true person we are to emerge.

I am defined by who I really am. Others may have their opinions, but I will stand up to my truth.

December 18

For fast-acting relief try slowing down.
LILY TOMLIN

We live in a global society. We can be anywhere these days with the internet and a flick of the computer mouse. We shop on-line. We order services on-line. We communicate with others on-line. We can even bank on-line. All so that we can pack more into our day than we used to. Instead of giving us some relief from the activities we try to fit into our day, it increases the amount of what we think we should be able to accomplish.

Simplify, simplify, simplify. That is the message we receive in recovery. Technology can even be used to support that message, not contradict it. We need to use whatever is available to us to simplify our life and leave it simplified. We'll get everything that is important to our well being done. We just need to look at our life and determine what is necessary and what we intentionally add in that ends up complicating our life and frustrating us. By understanding what is necessary and what is not, we create a life for ourselves that is full of peace and serenity. A life free of compulsive gambling.

Today, I will determine what is necessary for me and which activities I can eliminate. I will include only activities that support my serenity.

December 19

Obstacles don't have to stop you. If you run into a wall, don't turn around and give up. Figure out how to climb it, go through it, or work around it.

MICHAEL JORDAN

We face many obstacles on our road to recovery. Sometimes, it is people who don't want us to succeed in eliminating gambling from our life. They may try to tempt us back into gambling because they are fearful their relationship with us will change. What they don't understand is that our main relationship was not with them. It was with gambling. They may think that if we are successful in recovery, we won't have a place for them in our life. That may be true. We have to face that fact.

If we are to be successful, we have to face our obstacles head on. If we have people in our life who won't support us in our recovery efforts every step—and it is truly every step—of the way, we have to determine if there is a place for these people in our life. Are we better off with them or without them? If we want to move forward in recovery, we must remove anything that prevents us from accomplishing this. It is not a selfish act. Rather, it is a selfless act. We choose recovery. We choose serenity.

~

I will face my obstacles straight on. I will not allow obstacles to prevent me from working my program.

December 20

The greater the obstacle, the more glory in overcoming it."

MOLIERE

Every day we are bombarded with gambling ads. Television ads for casinos are calling to us to join them and win the big one. Radio commercials invite us to take the chance and buy a lottery ticket. Church events call on us to play bingo. Even fast food restaurants lure us with scratch off cards to win prizes.

Temptations are not going to go away. Each an every day we will be faced with temptations. We cannot eliminate them from our life. Our reaction to these obstacles, however, is what counts. Will we give in to seductive invitations? Or will we be able to recognize them for what they are—a hurdle for us to leap as we move forward on our path to recovery. As we grow stronger in our recovery process, the temptations become weaker to us. We will be able to listen to the commercials, but not hear them. They will simply become background noise to us as we proceed in peace.

~

I will not let temptations distract me from my real goal.
I will stay on my path to recovery.

December 21

How many cares one loses when one decides
not to be something, but to be someone.
COCO CHANEL

Comparisons can be deadly for us. Measuring ourselves against others' standards allows others to control our life. We feel we are inferior. We can't possibly live up to their standards. Feelings of unworthiness seep in. Feelings of failure haunt us.

We must remember that we are in charge of our life, not others. We are also in charge of the decision to look at our own life and make it the best possible or to use others lives as measuring sticks. By choosing to work our own program, we understand that others' lives are theirs to deal with. We have our own life that needs attention. It has been neglected for too long. In recovery, we know that the life we lead is worth having. The person we are is worth being. The feeling we experience are valid and real.

I am happy for the life I lead in recovery.
I am pleased to be me.

December 22

Perpetual optimism is a force multiplier.
COLIN POWELL

How is my outlook today? Full of doom and gloom? Ready to find any negative I can? Do I think the world is caving in on me because I am putting all my energy into my recovery program?

Sometimes we don't want to work our program. We're having a rough day. We might even have take a step backwards. It is a struggle for us to think about not gambling for the rest of our life.

The rule is don't think about it! The rest of our life is a long time away. Instead, we need to focus on the next minute. Take this tough day a minute at a time, if that is all we can manage. The important thing is that we pull ourselves up and take that first baby step for today. The other steps will come. If we work our recovery program, it won't give up on us. And, it won't allow us to give up on ourselves. We won't want to. We will know that our program offers us the only path to the joy we so dearly want.

Today, I am optimistic about my recovery.
I work my program knowing
I am secure in my growth.

December 23

I can positively see that this is a terrible day.

SUSAN B.

Attitude check. How am I doing? Do I look at my life and see nothing but doom and gloom? Or, am I able to realistically evaluate the wrongs I've done, the reasons and feelings behind them and understand that it was a place I left when I committed myself to my recovery program?

Attitude is a key component in our progress in recovery. Working our program with a positive attitude expands the possibilities for us. We can see the sunny days as we make progress in our program. We can work through the emotions we have held inside for so long with the knowledge that releasing them is good for us and our ability to take another step forward in recovery. The promise of peace and serenity is certainly worth all of the thorns we may step on along our route. Removing that thorn and stepping back on the path to walk that recovery road is another victory for us in working our program.

~

I will recognize that the thorns I step on
along my path to recovery are minor difficulties.
Removing the thorns and working through my issues
brings me peace.

December 24

To lead a symphony, you must occasionally turn your back on the crowd.

SAYING ON A PLAQUE

Our friends from our active gambling days may not understand the new, clean person we have become. They may not understand the new behaviors we have chosen. They may even resent the changes in our lives.

We might find that we have to make new choices in who we associate with. We need to involve ourselves with healthy people. People who resist compulsive gambling and work their program of recovery.

To live our program of serenity, we have to leave behind the people who may jeopardize our recovery. We can pray that they may find the way to the peace we have found.

~

I will surround myself with healthy people.
I am happy for the support I have in recovery.

December 25

When I grow up I want to be a little boy.

JOSEPH HELLER

Throughout our life, we've been mature beyond our years. We've had to deal with a life far beyond the years we were prepared for. We were told by adults in our life how to feel. Or, how not to feel. Our feelings were discounted. We were not allowed to experience our feelings. We were told we were wrong. We were shamed.

In recovery, we are not only allowed to feel our feelings, we are encouraged to. Working our program requires that we reach way down deep into ourselves to find those feelings we were shamed into hiding and bring them to the surface. When this happens, we can acknowledge our right to have our feelings and work through each and every one, step by step. We know that by dealing with our feelings openly we can release the cloud of shame we've lived under and open ourselves to a life of joy.

~

Although I am an adult, I have many
unreleased feelings from my childhood.
I will allow my feelings to come to the surface
so I can deal with them openly.

December 26

Begin somewhere.
You cannot build a reputation on what you intend to do.
LIZ SMITH

"I intend to stay free of my gambling addiction," states Teresa, "I will not gamble again."

"That's great," says Steve, "what are you doing to ensure you won't gamble?"

"Stay away from the casino, of course," said Teresa.

Teresa is on the right track. Certainly, staying away from her place of choice during her active gambling days is significant in her attempt to remain free of gambling. Her intention is in the right place.

The only chance for Teresa to succeed, though, is if her intention is part of a solid recovery program. How many times have we intended to stay away from gambling, only to return to our game of choice after a few days, a few weeks, or even a few months? We intended to stop gambling forever, but we couldn't.

Then, we admitted to ourselves and our Higher Power that we were helpless against our addiction. By working our recovery program with our Higher Power in control, we know we can stay away from gambling. Our intention becomes reality for us.

~

Today, I intend to choose recovery. I will work my program so that my intention becomes my reality.

December 27

It is never too late to be what you might have been.

GEORGE ELIOT

I'm forty years old," said Steve, "how much of a life do I have left? I've destroyed so much of my life up to now by gambling. What could possibly be left?"

If Steve was working his recovery program, he would know that today is left. For today is all that any of us have. Today is a gift to us. A gift that we can use to create the best day possible for ourselves in recovery. Today is a step towards a tomorrow that is free of gambling. We know that making it through today without gambling will set the foundation for any tomorrows that we are given by our Higher Power. If we do, indeed, have a tomorrow, a next week, a next year, we have the base for ensuring that by working our program we can remain free of the clutches of compulsive gambling.

~

Today is the day I will use to ensure
I work my program. To ensure I am setting
the foundation for my recovery.

December 28

Surround yourself with only people who are going to lift you higher.

OPRAH WINFREY

"I quit gambling, just like he wanted me to," cried Sally, "why is he now trying to undermine my efforts to stay clean? It seems all I do is struggle. First, with my gambling addiction. Then, with my recovery because he won't support me."

It certainly can be discouraging when our loved ones turn on us. Particularly if they were encouraging of our efforts to enter our recovery program in the first place. Why does it happen?

When we begin to work our program, changes begin to take place in us. It is more than just quitting gambling. That's certainly half of it. The other half is dealing with all of the issues and emotions that started us gambling in the first place. When that happens, loved ones see big changes in us. They begin getting frightened that we may not want them in our life. They might not have liked who we were while we were gambling, but as unpredictable as we were, we were predictable in our erratic behavior.

We cannot let that distract us from our work. We have to change in order for us to remain free from gambling.

I acknowledge that others in my life may struggle with my new found serenity. I remain solid in the knowledge that my program is working for me.

December 29

Life has a practice of living you, if you don't live it.
PHILIP LARKIN

Life happens. If we look around us, we see things going on all over the place. Sports teams play their games. Musicians are strumming their guitars. Traffic is racing past. People are scrambling from one place to the next. Phones are ringing. Activity is swirling on all sides of us.

The thing we have to be careful of is that we don't let life live us. We have only so many hours in each day. Twenty-four is all we get, no matter who we are. No more. No less. It is what we do with that precious time that makes a difference in whether we remain free from compulsive gambling or whether we allow ourselves to slip back into our addiction.

What will you do with your 24 hours today? Will you fill it up with activities that don't support your recovery? Or, will you filter out the distractions? Will you focus your attention on your responsibilities to your program? How will you spend your time?

~

I know I have only 24 hours each day.
I will use my day to further my progress in recovery.

December 30

You may be disappointed if you fail, but you are doomed if you don't try.

BEVERLY SILLS

Recovery isn't a cake walk. We can be diligently working our program. Then, an obstacle blocks our path. It may lure us back to gambling, even once. We feel like a failure. Is it possible that we'll never be able to remove these barriers that get in our way?

Sometimes we do move several steps ahead, only to take a step or two backwards. The key is to pick ourselves back up, brush ourselves off and take another step forward. Even a baby step will do. We all make mistakes. It doesn't mean we are a failure. It means we made a mistake. We must admit our error, forgive ourselves and get back on that path to recovery. That is what working our program is all about. By reaching out to our Higher Power, we can find the support we need to regain the strength we need to move forward again.

~

I know I will make mistakes in working my program.
I will forgive myself and get right back to working
my program with the assistance of my Higher Power.

December 31

It is best to learn as we go, not go as we have learned.

LESLIE JEANNE SAHLER

We have been taught many lessons throughout our life. As a child, we learned that we didn't count. We weren't allowed to have feelings. Crying was for sissys. Laughter mean we were making too much noise and had to quite down. Questioning anything was met with a quick slap across the mouth. Is it any wonder we grew up learning that anything we did was shameful? Is it a surprise that we felt we didn't count? Is it shocking to know why we turned to gambling for relief from the life that was so familiar to us?

Not at all. But the time to give that up is now. In recovery, we learn to "unlearn" the destructive lessons we've learned up to now. We learn that the loneliness and isolation we feel is legitimate. Working our program can help us work through those feelings of loneliness. It can help us face the isolation that kept us gambling head on. In recovery we find that we are valued by ourselves and others. We know that we count in this life. We learn what a wonderful feeling that is.

I will release the hurtful lessons I have learned.
I know the only lessons that are valuable to me
are those learned working my program.

INDEX OF TOPICS

Index of Authors